Praise for *Brilliant Teac*

'This is a brilliant "what you need to
range of information with practice ex
uable asset in any teaching assistant's toolkit.'

Karen Freeman, Teaching Assistant Course Lead/Lecturer, Northbrook College, West Sussex

'Packed with up to date and essential information to support teaching assistants; a must-have for anyone interested in being a TA.'

Penny Tassoni MBE, author, education consultant and trainer

'This book will support trainee teaching assistants and educators to understand the key themes in education. It provides context with examples and helpful case studies. The chapters are informative and accessible with clear, well-written sections. This book will help the readers to understand current subjects around supporting teaching and learning.'

Debra Brokenbrow, Lecturer in Education, Bath College

'An essential guide full of advice, case studies and dos and don'ts. Perfect for those new to, or considering joining, one of the most valuable school roles.'

Nadeem Qureshi, Class Teacher and Senior Leader, Chevening Primary School

Brilliant Teaching Assistant

Brilliant Teaching Assistant

What you need to know to be a truly outstanding teaching assistant

Second Edition

Louise Burnham

Harlow, England • London • New York • Boston • San Francisco • Toronto • Sydney
Dubai • Singapore • Hong Kong • Tokyo • Seoul • Taipei • New Delhi
Cape Town • São Paulo • Mexico City • Madrid • Amsterdam • Munich • Paris • Milan

PEARSON EDUCATION LIMITED
KAO Two
KAO Park
Harlow CM17 9NA
United Kingdom
Tel: +44 (0)1279 623623
Web: www.pearson.com

First published 2011 (print)
Second edition published 2024 (print and electronic)

ISBN: 978-1-292-46083-3 (print)
978-1-292-46082-6 (ePub)

British Library Cataloguing-in-Publication Data
A catalogue record for the print edition is available from the British Library

Library of Congress Cataloging-in-Publication Data
Names: Burnham, Louise, author.
Title: Brilliant teaching assistant : what you need to know to be a truly outstanding teaching assistant / Louise Burnham.
Description: Second edition. | Hoboken, NJ : Pearson, 2024. | Includes bibliographical references and index.
Identifiers: LCCN 2024006205 | ISBN 9781292460833 (paperback) | ISBN 9781292460826 (epub)
Subjects: LCSH: Teachers' assistants--Great Britain.
Classification: LCC LB2844.1.A8 B88 2024 | DDC 371.14/124--dc23/eng/20240213
LC record available at https://lccn.loc.gov/2024006205

10 9 8 7 6 5 4 3 2 1
28 27 26 25 24

Cover designer by Two Associates

Print edition typeset in 10/14 Charter ITC Pro by Straive
Print edition printed and bound in Ashford Colour Press Ltd, Gosport

NOTE THAT ANY PAGE CROSS REFERENCES REFER TO THE PRINT EDITION

For Brilliant Bonnie

Contents

While we work hard to present unbiased, fully accessible content, we want to hear from you about any concerns or needs with this Pearson product so that we can investigate and address them:

- Please contact us with concerns about any potential bias at https://www.pearson.com/report-bias.html
- For accessibility-related issues, such as using assistive technology with Pearson products, alternative text requests, or accessibility documentation, email the Pearson Disability Support team at **disability.support@pearson.com**

About the author

Louise Burnham is a teacher, assessor and qualifications developer. She has worked in education for thirty years, both in primary schools and further education colleges. Her roles in schools have included senior management as EYFS manager as well that of SENDCo. She led teaching assistant training in a south London college for many years and currently continues to teach part time in a primary school as well as working as an assessor and advisor for teaching assistants and students of early years, and volunteering for a local toddler group.

She has written over 20 books for early years and teaching assistant students and her name is well known in these areas as a result, particularly for the textbooks for Supporting Teaching and Learning at levels 2 and 3.

Author acknowledgements

The author would like to thank Eloise Cook, Rebecca Youe and Yashmeena Bisht for all their support with this project. In addition she would like to acknowledge the support of all the colleagues, students and pupils who continue to stimulate and inspire her every day.

Publisher's acknowledgements

Text Credits

3 Pearson Education: Burnham, L. (2007) S/NVQ Level 3 The Teaching Assistant's Handbook: Primary Schools; **18** UK Department of Education: The National Curriculum in England, December 2014. Department for Education.; **112** UK Department of Education: Special educational needs and disability code of practice, Jan 2015, Department for Education.; **112** UK Department of Education: Special educational needs and disability code of practice, Jan 2015, Department for Education.; **229** Pearson Education: Burnham, L. (2007) S/NVQ Level 3 The Teaching Assistant's Handbook: Primary Schools.

Image Credits

89 Shutterstock: Quang Vinh Tran / Shutterstock.

Introduction

Why become a teaching assistant?

'We get all the best bits!'

'We get to spend time with the children and have time to talk to them.'

'We are helping to shape the next generation.'

'It's great, it's fun and I can just go into work and go home again without having to do too much preparation.'

'I have always wanted to work with children and have never had the opportunity to do it until now. I love it!'

'It's great to be in the school environment and we don't have the same pressure as teachers.'

All of the above quotes were given by teaching assistants working in schools. If you have bought this book, you are interested in finding out whether you are or could become a Brilliant Teaching Assistant. This may be for a number of reasons:

- because you are interested in becoming a teaching assistant or are new to the role

- because you would like to find out more about the similarities and differences between jobs and schools
- because you may be thinking about taking the plunge and going back into work or training after a career break.

Alternatively, you may be quite experienced and want to find out more about different aspects of what teaching assistants do and broaden your horizons even further. Whatever your reasons, you will want to look at the range of opportunities available to you and consider how teaching assistants can really make a difference to pupils in many ways. From supporting teaching and learning in the classroom to mentoring, running intervention groups and providing a listening ear to pupils, teaching assistants are a vital part of the whole school team.

Support staff have always been in schools, but in 2002 the government started to give large amounts of funding to 'professionalising' their role and making specific qualifications available. According to data released by the Department for Education, the total number of teaching assistants in local authority-maintained English schools was 79,000 in 2000. At the time of writing in 2023 it stands at 281,094 (www.gov.uk, education statistics 2022). The impact of this has been huge and has meant that in some schools, the number of teaching assistants is now almost as high as the number of teachers.

Teaching assistants are now qualified and experienced to different levels, from Levels 2 and 3 (equivalent to GCSE and A level) in Supporting Teaching and Learning in Schools, to Higher Level Teaching Assistants (HLTAs) who may take whole classes and act as cover supervisors. T levels in Education and Childcare now offer a specialism in Assisting Teaching which may be studied by 16- to 18-year-olds. Teaching assistants may also have additional qualifications in areas of special educational needs and disabilities (SEND), so that they can work with specific pupils. This means that they will often have precise responsibilities, be part of a curriculum area, or have to plan, teach and assess pupils independently whilst reporting back to teachers.

No longer simply an 'extra pair of hands' in the classroom, teaching assistants are now an essential part of the school team and one which most teachers can seldom do without. Although this change has been gradual, the different roles which have evolved are now hugely varied and assistants are now taken on with widely differing job descriptions – something which would not have happened 25 years ago. Teaching assistants may work in a number of different roles in one school or have different jobs in different places. Consider the examples below:

Brilliant examples

Adjana

Adjana works in a large inner city secondary school alongside 20 other teaching assistants and individual support assistants (ISAs). She has a Maths degree and works closely with the Maths teacher, preparing resources and supporting both gifted and talented groups in the lower school and those working below age expectations in Years 10 and 11.

Carole

Carole works in a two-form entry primary academy and supports the class teacher in Year 1 during the mornings. She arrives at school at 8.45 and speaks briefly to the teacher before working alongside small groups for literacy. She then spends afternoons with different year groups as she supports the ICT technician and various class teachers. This gives her the opportunity to develop her interest in ICT.

Ian

Ian works in a small village primary school. He arrives at school at 7.30 and helps with breakfast club until school starts. He then works in Year 6 supporting literacy and numeracy groups in the morning before covering lunchtime. He then goes home. After school he comes back to work with after-school club.

Sanjay

Sanjay works in a private primary school and is an HLTA. He is the line manager for all the other teaching assistants in the school as well as working in Years 2 and 5, and running intervention groups. He is in charge of setting the playground and lunchtime duty rotas as well as running a football club after school.

Whatever your role, you will need to be able to turn your hand to most things in school – this may be anything from dealing with an injured or distressed pupil to invigilating exams or organising costumes for the Christmas play. However, as you become more experienced you will probably find there are some areas you are more comfortable with and be able to express your interest so that you can widen your experience. This is one of the great advantages of your job – you should be able to develop areas in which you have a particular strength or enthusiasm! This book will guide you through these different aspects of your role and also those of others in your school team so that you can see how you fit into the school as a whole. It also provides Brilliant case studies in each chapter, the solutions to which can be found in Appendix 1.

The term 'parents' in this book refers to all those who give primary care to children, including carers, foster parents and wider families.

Chapter 1

Working effectively as part of the whole school team

When you first start your new job or training you may be bewildered by the different titles which exist to describe the role of a teaching assistant. You may be known as an Individual Support Assistant, Learning Support Assistant, Special Support Assistant or Classroom Assistant. If you have a higher level qualification you may be employed as a Higher Level Teaching Assistant (HLTA). Although these are all slightly different, 'teaching assistant' is the generic term to cover all the different aspects of the role. In some schools and local authorities, those with different qualifications are given titles according to the level they have reached, but this is regional and will depend on where you are in the country. Whatever your role, it is important that you understand where and how you fit into the school team, so that you can maximise your effectiveness and that of those around you.

Teaching assistant terms

Teaching assistant	The generic term for anyone who supports teaching and learning in schools.
Classroom assistant	As above, anyone who supports teaching and learning in schools.
Individual Support Assistant (ISA)	This means that the assistant is allocated to work with a particular child, for example those who have special educational needs or disabilities (sometimes also called additional needs).
Learning Support Assistant/Special Support Assistant	As above, an assistant working with a named child who has additional needs.
Bilingual assistants	May work with pupils who do not speak the target language (i.e. English or Welsh). It may be necessary to use the pupil's first language to support them and to help assess their educational abilities. Bilingual assistants may also work with families and liaise with them in order to promote pupil participation.
Learning mentor	This role has evolved as usually a teaching assistant who works closely with a pupil in order to overcome barriers to learning. They will usually work as a listener, role model and advisor to pupils.
HLTA	A teaching assistant who has achieved higher level teaching assistant status.

What is a 'whole school' team?

There have been many models and breakdowns of how school teams fit together, and each school will be different, depending on whether it is a primary, secondary or special school, an academy, or an independent or international school, and how teams are managed within this. However, broadly speaking, all schools will have a governing body and a senior management team which supervises a team of teachers and teaching assistants along with other support staff. Within the different teams, line managers will exist for staff and you will need to know who yours is: as a teaching assistant it is unlikely that your line manager will be the headteacher – it is more likely to be the deputy headteacher, Special Educational Needs and Disabilities Co-ordinator (SENDCo) or possibly an HLTA.

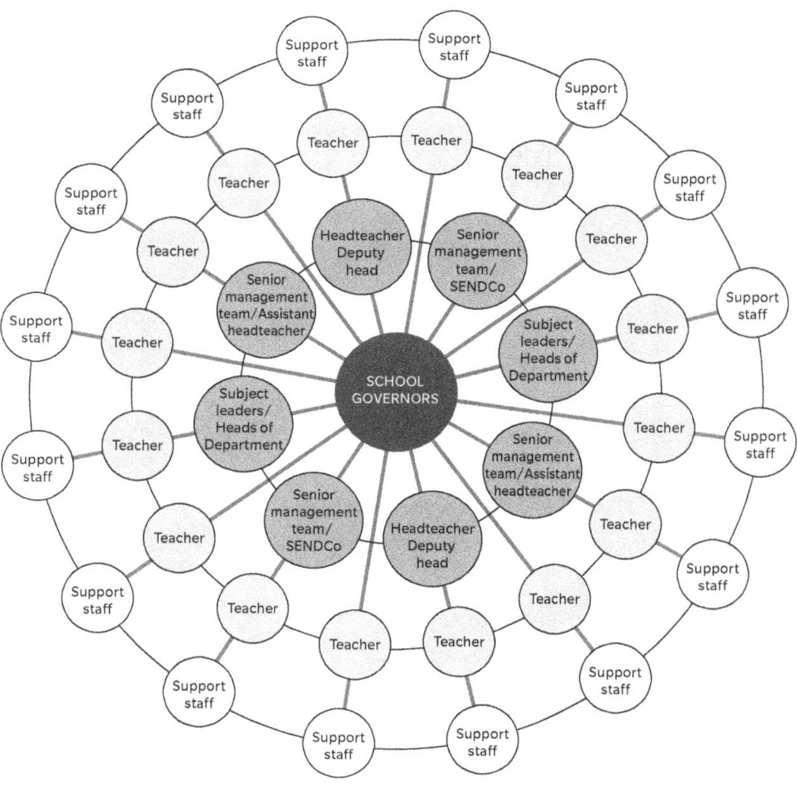

Figure 1.1 Support staff are part of the whole school team
Source: Burnham, L. (2007) *S/NVQ Level 3 The Teaching Assistant's Handbook: Primary Schools*

The governing body

Historically, the governing body of a school will be made up of a team of around ten or twelve people who meet regularly and have close contact with the headteacher and senior management team. They will usually have areas of expertise which may be in the financial, legal or business world and will be from the local community. There will also be staff and parent governors – if you have time and you are interested in becoming a governor this is worth doing as it gives a real insight into how the school is run.

The governing body will also be responsible for carrying out the headteacher's performance management interview. He or she will report to governors about the running of the school and is answerable to them about all aspects of it from financial management, site management, community cohesion and the curriculum, to employing new staff. With this in mind, the governing body will be split into different committees of around four members and will meet once or twice a term. They will then feed back to the main governing body once a term. Minutes of these meetings should be available to all staff and parents and carers if requested. The headteacher will also produce an annual report to them about what has been achieved during the previous year. Governors may be completely invisible to you but they should really make themselves known to all staff and children and should come regularly into school during the school day to see it in action rather than just in the evenings for meetings, although this may be difficult in reality due to other commitments.

In recent years, many schools have become academies and have become part of a local Multi Academy Trust (MAT) with other local schools. This means that several academies will come under one 'umbrella' and will share a CEO, an executive headteacher and a board of trustees. This is known as a Multi Academy Trust Board. However, each academy can also choose to retain its own governing body (usually known as local governors) if it feels that this is in the best interest of the school.

The Senior Management Team (SMT)

In all schools this team will meet regularly with the headteacher and deputy to discuss priorities in the school and to identify current issues in the school development plan (the school development plan or school improvement plan is a document which usually spans four or five years and sets out the overall priorities and plans for the school). You should be aware of who the senior managers are in your school and what their responsibilities are. The team will usually include the headteacher, deputies or assistant headteachers, the SENDCo, and year group or subject leaders, but may also include other managers, for example the foundation stage manager, if you are in a primary school, or head of sixth form in a secondary school. Senior managers will support the headteacher in decisions concerning the school and will ensure that information is passed on to all staff.

The SENCo or SENDCo

The SENCo or SENDCo (Special Educational Needs and Disabilities Co-ordinator) is responsible for managing the provision for pupils with special educational needs. They will need to meet and liaise with staff, as well as parents or carers and outside agencies, and may be your line manager if you are working as an individual support assistant. (For more on the role of the SENDCo see Chapter 6.)

Year group/Key stage leaders

Year group or key stage leaders are found both in primary and secondary schools, and are literally the lead teacher in that year group or key stage. They will usually be a member of the senior management team and will feed back information to their year group or key stage at their own meetings, usually weekly. Year group and key stage leaders will usually be the most experienced permanent members of staff in that team and so will be able to advise and support others in the team. They will also give guidance towards planning and assessment and make sure that resources are available to all. This may be an issue in a primary school where several classes in a year group are working on the same topic, or in a secondary school where different classes are covering the same areas of the curriculum at the same time.

Subject leaders/Heads of Department

These are teachers within both primary and secondary schools who have responsibility for a subject area or department. They will need to advise and support other staff in the planning, assessment, resourcing and teaching of the subject area. They will also need to monitor how it is taught in school and may carry out lesson observations or ask how things are going. They may also be useful to identify as you may be able to seek advice from them if you work regularly with a particular subject. As well as giving advice to staff within the school, subject leaders may also be involved at local authority level or within a group of academies in working with other schools to develop their subject area. They will probably attend local meetings to keep up to date with any developments in their subject area so that they can feed these back to school staff. Teaching assistants may also work closely with subject leaders or heads of department if they are specialists in a particular area, as is sometimes the case in secondary schools.

Teachers

Depending on whether you are in a primary, secondary or special school, the role of the teacher may vary considerably. Teachers in primary schools will be responsible for organising their classroom environment and for the planning, delivery and assessment of lessons in line with pupils' individual needs. In secondary schools, although they will have a class of pupils, they will be subject based and will not have such close contact with pupils and the parents or carers of pupils in their class. They will be responsible for the planning, delivery and assessment of classes within their subject area. In special schools, teachers may have much smaller classes at both primary and secondary level and there is likely to be a higher ratio of support staff to manage pupils' needs effectively.

Support staff

This will usually be quite a large group of people and although you will be part of it, depending on the size of your school, you may not meet with a wider group than other teaching assistants. However, support staff are made up of all other non-teaching staff in schools – that is office or admin staff, site managers, kitchen staff, ICT technicians, business managers, midday supervisors and others. Support staff will sometimes be part time and if you are also in school only on certain days you may not know everyone. If not, it will help to try to get to know others on occasions where everyone is in school such as INSET days, or perhaps at more social school events when these take place.

As well as the above broad headings, you will probably find that there are smaller sub-groups, for example midday supervisors, or early career teachers (ECTs, formerly NQTs), who may meet together or spend more time with one another than the wider group.

Brilliant example

David is an individual support assistant (ISA) in a secondary school. He is new to the role and is line-managed by the school's SENDCo. He has meetings with different teams within the school:

- David meets with the SENDCo both to discuss the pupils he works with and to clarify anything which comes up as he settles into school.
- He also meets with other ISAs and teaching assistants once a fortnight at lunchtime to find out about whole school issues.
- Occasionally, the whole school staff will meet together for staff training or INSET days.

Whatever teams or groups you are in, you should be able to contribute to their effectiveness and work alongside others for the benefit of pupils. You will also need to be able to contribute in your own way to the development of the team through providing support and advice to others. If you are lucky enough to work in a school where all staff members work together positively, you will find this very supportive to you in your role.

Brilliant tip

If you are new to a school, take a few moments to work out your own school's staff structure and who in the school is responsible for different areas. The office or school website will probably have a staff list which will identify names for you. Make sure you know who the key members of staff are and those who may be particularly relevant for you. Some schools will even have handy photographs of key staff on the wall in the entrance area, which, although useful, is not always popular! If you are part of a MAT, find out the names of other schools and key staff within your academy trust as well.

Working with others

Working with others will include how you relate to parents or carers, teachers and other school staff, as well as staff in other schools who are in your MAT. You may also work closely with other external professionals who visit the school, for example occupational therapists or speech therapists. (For more on this, see Chapter 6.)

As you will be working in different teams it is worth thinking about how your role fits in with others and how you are able to support them.

Depending on your experience, you will bring a unique level of expertise to your school or group of schools. You may have had specific training and be able to advise others. If you have information or expertise which would benefit others in your team, you should support them by passing on anything which may be useful. In some schools you may be required to feed back information on courses you have attended through meetings, or if you are experienced, you may be working with others who would benefit from some of your ideas – this could also be done more informally.

You may be less experienced and find that you are in a situation where you need advice and support – do not be afraid of asking for it. There will usually be someone in school who has dealt with a similar situation or who may put a different slant on things.

Brilliant case study

Emma has just spent break talking to Lorraine, who is another teaching assistant working in key stage 3. She has found some challenges in her work with a particular pupil whom Lorraine supported the previous year. Lorraine is able to talk through some of the strategies which worked and which she may find useful.

- In what ways will this chat be useful?
- How else might Lorraine be able to help Emma long term?

Working with other support staff within the same classroom

This may be surprising, but you might find yourself working in a class where there are a number of different support staff who have varying roles. An example of this might be in a classroom where there is more than one pupil who has an area of special educational need. Although extra support is always beneficial for the pupil, it may at times be difficult for adults to know exactly what their role is. It will be necessary in this situation to meet with teachers, the SENDCo or the other individuals concerned and talk through how pupils are supported within the class on a regular basis. You should also discuss how much time you should spend with the individual pupil on specific targets and how much time you can spend on group work. This is particularly important where more than one assistant is working with a pupil (e.g. if one person is with them in the morning and another in the afternoon).

Working alongside teachers

This really is the key part of your role. You will need to be able to get the best out of the time available with the staff with whom you are working so that you can work together for the benefit of pupils. At the beginning of each term it would be useful to sit down with key staff and plan out whether you will have time to meet, what kind of information would be useful to you and how you might best work together in your particular situation. Some teaching assistants literally have no time to plan with or talk to teachers and will walk into class on a regular basis with no idea what is being taught that day – this is clearly not ideal for anyone. In these circumstances it would make sense for teachers to email plans to teaching assistants if time is not available – at least then the lesson or support required will not be a surprise on the day. You should also have the opportunity to feed back to teachers on how pupils you have supported have worked during lessons and whether they have met the learning objectives so that they are able to plan effectively for next time – again, if this is not possible in the time available you may consider using feedback forms or annotated lesson plans. (See also Chapter 3 for more on working with teachers.)

Working with parents or carers

All staff working in schools will need to be able to relate to parents or carers. Although their main point of contact will be teachers, if you are working as a teaching assistant you may well have regular meetings or points of contact with them, particularly if you support an individual child, such as a pupil with special educational needs or a bilingual pupil. You should make sure that you stay on subject when talking to parents or carers and that you are mindful of confidentiality issues (discussed later in this chapter) and remain professional. It is also important not to take things into your own hands; if you think that the parent or carer has asked something which is more appropriate for a teacher to deal with, you must say so and refer to them. Don't be drawn into something which you do not feel confident in discussing, particularly if you don't know about it.

Managing conflict

Working with others, in whatever profession you choose, will sometimes be great and at others difficult and you are bound to get on with some people more than others. At some point in your career, it is likely that you will find yourself having to work with a personality which may be very different from your own. This may be a teacher or manager but it is also possible that you will have to work regularly with another professional, or a parent, who you find it hard to relate to. If you anticipate finding them hard to work with, it is important to remember that it is probably for a relatively short time and that you may well learn a lot by working with that person. You should remain professional at all times and where issues arise in the workplace, talk them through with the relevant person, such as your line manager.

You will also need to be sensitive at times to others' needs – all members of staff in schools will have a lot on their mind and you may not be aware what pressures they are under as part of their job. Many will have families and issues to deal with outside school, which at times can also have an impact on their ability to provide the same level of support. You should also try to be self-aware and think about the way in which you relate to others in your team, as it may be that you do not come across in the way that you think. If someone is not reacting to you in a positive way, could it be because of something you have said to them?

If you find yourself in a conflict situation with another individual this will need to be addressed as soon as possible. Although rare, these issues do occasionally happen and you may need to have a meeting with another adult present in order to discuss a way forward. Be particularly careful if you are alone with another person – if you are not comfortable, and the other person is being aggressive or abusive in some way, move to a different place or tell them that you are not prepared to discuss the situation without a mediator. If the conflict is more of a low-level disagreement and is ongoing, you should always seek additional help and refer to your school's grievance policy.

As an adult in a school environment, you must remember that you are responsible for being a role model and showing pupils positive relationships. Pupils will witness how adults interact with one another and work together and will take their lead from them. If they see adults being considerate and appreciative of others it is far more likely that they will behave in the same way.

Remembering confidentiality

When you start your job it is likely that your line manager or head-teacher will speak to you about the importance of confidentiality in school. This is particularly relevant to you as a teaching assistant because in many cases teaching assistants are also parents or carers, often of pupils in the same school. The most important thing to remember is not to speak about pupils or staff to those who do not work in the school, and if in doubt about whether you should say something – don't!

Brilliant case study

Sina works in a small village primary school as a teaching assistant in Year 2. Her child is in another class and her best friend is also a parent at the school. Sina's friend regularly tries to find out what happens in the class on a daily basis and often questions her on the way home about specific children. She is also very keen that her child is put up to the next level in reading and asks Sina to 'sort it out' for her.

- What should Sina do in this situation?
- Why is it important that she does not talk to her friend about what happens in class?

Brilliant dos and don'ts

Do

✔ Embrace differences – it would be very boring if we were all the same!

✔ Acknowledge the support and ideas of others.

✔ Always try to talk disagreements through rationally as they arise.

✔ Try to attend the occasional staff social event.

Don't

✗ Get caught up in an argument, particularly in front of pupils.

✗ Gossip or talk about others negatively in the workplace.

✗ Breach confidentiality.

School policies

All schools are required to have a number of different policies which are designed to support the smooth running of the school. These will be divided into curriculum and non-curriculum areas and should be revised and updated on a regular basis. Your line manager will be able to tell you where you need to go to refer to them, probably in the school office, and they should be on the school's website so that parents and carers can look at them easily. Everyone who works in the school should also be aware of where to find them and should have some idea about the content of each. A list of some of the policies which you should know about and be able to find are given below:

- health and safety policy
- behaviour policy
- safeguarding policy
- prevent policy

- GDPR and data protection policy
- marking policy
- inclusion/equal opportunities and diversity policy

You should also know your school's SEND policy if you are working with pupils who have special educational needs or disabilities, foundation stage or early years policy if you are working in Reception, and so on. If you are working in a specific curriculum area, for example in the history department, you should ensure that you have read the appropriate curriculum policy. Your line manager will be able to talk to you about anything which may need clarification.

Brilliant activity

Find out what you can about the Prevent Duty Guidance 2023 and what it means for schools.

Brilliant tip

Be aware of where the school keeps its policies so that you can refer to them when necessary.

Brilliant recap

- All schools will be structured in a similar way but within this there may be slight differences.
- There will be a number of different teams within the whole school structure and you may be part of more than one of these – e.g. subject area or department, support staff teams, year group or key stage teams. Make sure you know where you fit in.
- Remember when working with others to be professional at all times and observe confidentiality.

References

The Prevent Duty: Advice for schools and childcare providers 2023: Schools must have regard to the Prevent Duty Guidance 2023 which aims to prevent pupils from being drawn into terrorism.

Chapter 2

Understanding the school curriculum, timetabling and planning

As a member of staff who supports teaching and learning, you will need to have some awareness of the curriculum you are supporting, its structure and how different types of planning fit together. Although different areas of the curriculum may undergo changes from time to time, the principle of knowing and understanding the key areas of learning in whatever subject area you are supporting remains just as important and you should be entitled to additional training if the curriculum of the age group or key stage you are supporting changes radically.

Whilst some teaching assistants may be closely involved in planning with teachers, others may have no input, sight of plans or idea about what they will be doing until they are asked to support teaching and learning activities with individuals or groups on the day. You will need to try to work with teachers to ensure that you know as much as possible in advance about the lessons you will be supporting so that all pupils have full access to the curriculum for their age and stage.

The School Curriculum 4–16

The National Curriculum

In 1988, the Education Reform Act changed the way in which the curriculum was delivered in England and Wales when the government introduced a National Curriculum. This was designed so that all state schools would have guidance as to the content of what was expected to be taught and for ease of planning and assessment.

Since 1988 the curriculum has been through some changes and is regularly updated, and different countries of the UK now have their own distinct curricula. However, in England the National Curriculum at primary and secondary level is divided into specific subjects which are both statutory and non-statutory.

The National Curriculum is statutory in all state schools and whilst the various subject areas are important, the document states that 'the National Curriculum is just one element in the education of every child' *(National Curriculum Introduction, 2014)*. The document also covers aspects of education which support a pupil's overall development and general achievement. These are areas such as Citizenship and Personal, social and health education (sometimes known as PSHE or PSE) – economic well-being, sex education, careers education and so on. Although these areas are non-statutory they are an important part of the pupil's school experience as they will enhance learning and development.

Brilliant example

As part of the non-statutory curriculum, a primary school has a school council in which elected representatives from each year group meet every half term to discuss issues which have been suggested by children in the school. They then feed this back to the teaching staff so that they can act on them as well as raising awareness of the children's concerns. An example of this was their wish to reduce plastic waste within the school and encourage pupils to recycle as much as possible, for example when bringing drinks containers to school.

From Year 1 onwards, the National Curriculum is comprised of:

- key stage 1 (Years 1 and 2 – sometimes still called 'infants')
- key stage 2 (Years 3, 4, 5 and 6 – sometimes still called 'juniors')

At secondary school, the curriculum is set out in different stages:

- key stage 3 – Years 7–9
- key stage 4 – Years 10 and 11
- post-16 (sixth form)

National Curriculum subjects – Primary (Key stages 1 and 2)

Compulsory subjects are:

- English
- mathematics
- science
- computing
- geography
- history
- art and design
- music
- physical education (PE), including swimming
- design and technology; and
- ancient and modern foreign languages at key stage 2

As well as these compulsory subjects, primary schools must also provide relationships and health education (RSE) and religious education (RE). In the case of RE, parents and carers can request that their child is taken out of all or part of a lesson.

In addition, schools will also often teach:

- personal, social and health education (PSHE)
- citizenship
- foreign languages in key stage 1
- puberty and sex education

In the case of sex education, parents and carers can also request that their child is taken out of the lesson.

National Curriculum subjects – Secondary (Key stages 3 and 4)

- English
- citizenship
- computing
- mathematics
- physical education
- science
- religious education

In addition, key stage 3 only:

- art and design
- modern foreign languages
- design and technology
- history
- geography
- music

Schools must also provide relationships and sex education (RSE) at key stages 3 and 4.

With the exception of religious education, which is planned locally, each subject is broken down into programmes of study for each key stage and lists the knowledge, skills and understanding which are expected of each pupil in different areas. For example, in primary English, learning is divided into four areas: spoken language, reading, writing and spelling, vocabulary, punctuation and grammar. These areas then have headings about what should be taught at each key stage and by year group.

Brilliant example

Year 3 pupils are required to learn about light in science. They follow the programme of study as defined by the National Curriculum under the subject list and then science at key stage 2.

Look at the requirements for teaching light in Year 3 and again in Year 6. What progress can you see between the beginning and end of key stage 2? How useful do you think the National Curriculum is as a resource?

The Early Years Foundation Stage/Early Years Framework

Depending on your country of the UK, the curriculum for the early years may be given a different heading or title and may extend to a different age. The Early Years Foundation Stage (EYFS) is the statutory curriculum framework which is used in Nursery and Reception classes and in childcare settings for children up to five years in England.

In Wales, the early years are covered by their Curriculum for Wales, which encompasses this phase of learning (from ages 3 to 16).

During this phase, children's learning is focused around five developmental pathways rather than the six areas of learning which are part of the curriculum for older children. The five developmental pathways are:

- belonging
- communication
- exploration
- physical development
- wellbeing

In Scotland and Northern Ireland, there are also separate curricula which focus on the needs of pupils who are at the earlier stages of learning. In Scotland, the curriculum is focused around the document 'A Curriculum for Excellence – building the Curriculum 3–18'. The curriculum for 3- to 5-year-olds and the early primary phase (Primary 1) are presented as one level. This means that, although in Scotland there is a distinction between the phases, children only start to have more formal teaching when they are ready. There is also a strong emphasis on active learning and on deepening pupils' knowledge.

In Scotland, the early years curriculum is distinct from the rest of the curriculum in England and Wales in that it is divided into eight areas of learning, which are:

- language and literacy
- mathematics and numeracy
- religious and moral education
- science
- social studies
- technology
- expressive arts
- health and wellbeing

In Northern Ireland, the early years or pre-school curriculum is divided into the following areas:

- personal, social and emotional development
- physical development
- creative/aesthetic development
- language development
- early mathematical experiences
- early experiences in science and technology
- knowledge and appreciation of the environment

In England, the seven areas of learning are divided into prime and specific areas of learning. Children will need to develop a strong foundation in the three prime areas so that they are able to move on to strengthen their knowledge and understanding in the four specific areas.

Prime areas of learning:

- communication and language
- physical development
- personal, social and emotional development

Specific areas of learning:

- literacy
- mathematics
- understanding of the world
- expressive arts and design

These seven areas of learning broadly cover other curriculum subjects which children will study from key stage 1 onwards; for example computing and science will be incorporated under understanding of the world, and art and music under expressive arts and design. Under each of these areas of learning there will then be early learning goals, which set out the expected end of stage level of attainment before children go into Year 1. British International schools will also usually follow the English EYFS.

The way in which learning is usually managed in the early years is that adults work alongside children on focused activities that involve specific concepts, such as using numbers or the development of writing or language activities. Children also work independently and self-select from a wide range of activities within and outside the classroom which encourage them to develop their autonomy and independence whilst developing their knowledge and skills. These will include activities such as messy play, sensory activities, cutting and sticking, painting, use of writing corner, role play, sand and water and so on.

At this stage of learning you will also be supporting pupils as they settle into school, as well as preparing them to move up to key stage 1 at the end of Reception.

Although not part of the curriculum, it is important that these transition phases are managed well so that children feel confident and secure in their new environments. You will need to be able to do the following:

- encourage and promote children's independence
- take time to talk to children and get to know them individually
- make sure that activities take account of children's needs
- gradually integrate them into the life of the school

(See also Chapter 4 on providing pastoral support to pupils.)

If you are working with this age group in school and have not done so before, you should have some additional advice and support through your school as there are differences in the way the early years curriculum is planned and assessed, and it is less formal than the curriculum in other year groups.

Brilliant case study

Myra is working in a small one form entry primary school and usually floats between Years 1 and 2. The teaching assistant who has worked in the Reception class for the last few years has gone on maternity leave and as cover is needed, Myra has been asked to step in for a few months. She does not have experience of the EYFS and soon starts to feel that she needs more support from her school.

- Where should Myra go for support in the first instance?
- Is there anywhere else Myra could seek help?

Brilliant tip

If you are working with this age group, make sure you have seen a copy of the practice guidance for the early years curriculum in your home country. This will give you clear guidelines for what is expected of pupils and how they should be assessed.

Timetables

The way in which teachers plan their timetables at the early years stage will depend on the structure of the school day. For example, the timings of breaks, lunchtimes and assemblies, as well as the use of rooms such as halls and outside areas may depend on when they are being used by other classes or depend on routines and staffing. Usually, children of this age do not have playtimes and assemblies with the rest of the school, particularly when they are very new to the school environment. As foundation stage classes will have their own outside area and the way in which their day is structured will be different, this should not be necessary in any case. It is important for young children to have set routines although these will still need to be flexible due to the needs of this age group.

Brilliant case study

Tina has just got a job supporting a Reception teacher working in a small school. In her first job as a teaching assistant, she was at a larger primary where the Reception and Nursery classes worked together as a unit for the foundation stage and did not have much contact with the rest of the school, particularly as they were housed in a separate building. In her new job, the school does not have a Nursery, and the Reception class are expected to join in far more with whole school activities such as assemblies. Tina is surprised by the difference and is quite unsettled as a result, as she is not sure that it is appropriate for this age group.

- Do you think that this could be a problem?
- Should Tina say anything?

Timetabling for older pupils will follow a more familiar structure and will usually be taught by subject although where there are opportunities these may well overlap, for example if pupils are working on graphs on the computers as part of their mathematics, or in primary school being taught by topic. The way in which you support learners may vary according to timetable and present different challenges, particularly in secondary schools where you may have to get from one end of the school to another between lessons, or have fewer opportunities to meet with teachers.

In special schools, timetables may be specific to individual pupils rather than classes but this will depend on the type of school and the needs of the children.

Planning

As you are working with teachers on a daily basis it is useful to understand the way in which long-term planning takes place and how plans fit together in the medium and short term. Although formats may be different from school to school and teacher to teacher, the basics are likely to be the same, and some may be more visible than others. Plans are usually written some time in advance, and will at the earliest stages take the form of long-, medium- and finally short-term plans (see Table 2.1).

Brilliant example

Habiba works as a teaching assistant in the maths department of a large secondary school where maths is based in specific classrooms. In her school, teachers are required to put medium- and short-term plans for Years 7–9 on the classroom wall so that all adults in the room can refer to them.

Rob works in Year 3 and 4 of a small primary school and moves between classrooms running intervention groups for phonics. Some of the teachers have plans ready for him on a Monday and others give them to him on the day.

- Long-term plans: these are usually for the whole year – they may also be called schemes of work.
- Medium-term plans: these are for the term or half term and set out the progression within each plan.
- Short-term plans: these are for the week or day and will incorporate learning objectives and state how the class or group will be organised.

It could be that teachers plan for the long and medium term and that you are involved in short-term or daily plans, or plans for individual sessions. Ideally, you and teachers should plan together so that you are clear from the outset what you will be doing and will have had the opportunity to put forward your own ideas. In the case of teaching assistants who support individual pupils, this can be particularly beneficial since you will be able to identify any difficulties with planned activities at the earliest stages and will also know in

Table 2.1 The three different types of planning

Stage of planning	Purpose	Content
Long term (curriculum framework)	Shows coverage of subject and provides breadth.	Summary of subject content.
Medium term (termly or half termly)	Provides a framework for all subjects.	Shows overview of activities and/ or topics. Links to national strategies.
Short term	Provides a plan for the week's lessons, which can be broken down by day.	Should include: • learning intentions • activities • organisation/ differentiation • provision for SEND • use of other adults • rough time allocations • space for notes

advance if particular resources are needed. In secondary schools, you will need to have contact with teachers you are supporting so that you can find out about planning in advance; due to time this may need to be via email.

Plans should not be a secret and creating them is part of the teacher's role; if it is difficult for you to see them in advance, and this is a problem, keep trying to find out how it may be possible for you to see them before the lesson. You and the teacher are both there to

Brilliant tip

If you do not have time to plan with teachers, ask them to email plans to you when they are completed so that you are able to look through them before lessons.

support pupil learning – neither of you can do your job effectively if you have no time to communicate with one another.

Whatever plan you are following or lesson you are supporting, you should know the learning objectives so that you and the pupils are clear about what they will be expected to have achieved by the end of the session. This is true of pupils of any age; for example if you are working with early years children you can still tell them verbally 'today we are learning to. . .' whilst with older pupils the learning objective should be displayed and discussed at the start of each lesson. If pupils are not informed about the purpose of their learning they are less likely to be engaged in the lesson. In addition, many schools now use assessment for learning (for more on this see Chapter 3) as a means of encouraging pupils to be part of the assessment process. This has become a regularly used motivational way of encouraging pupils of all ages to take responsibility for their own learning. It is a way of ensuring that learners are clear on the purpose of what they are doing, what they need to do and how close they are to achieving it.

Brilliant example: An RE lesson plan for Year 5

Learning objective: I know some of the key facts about Judaism and Sukkot.

- In small groups on large paper the children should create a mind map of everything they know about Jews, Judaism, being Jewish and share as a class – what questions would you ask a Jewish person visiting our school?
- Groups to share ideas with the class: make a list of appropriate vocabulary on the board.
- Tell pupils that over the next few weeks we will be learning about Sukkot, a Jewish festival. Tell pupils why it is celebrated. Give children the 'key facts' sheet on Sukkot and

ask them to make notes as you talk it through. TA to support blue table with this.

- Assessment for learning opportunity– go through what they have learned about Sukkot – peer assess – do their notes reflect this?

Keep their large sheets of paper so that we can compare their knowledge at the end of the unit.

At the early years level, plans may take the form of topic-based ideas so that learning can be linked to a particular theme. For example, the popular topic of transport in Reception classes can encompass each of the seven areas of learning (see fig 2.1 on page 31).

For more on planning and assessment see Chapter 3.

Brilliant dos and don'ts – Planning

Do

✔ Get involved with planning as much as you can.

✔ Ask to see any long-term plans as these will need to be done well in advance.

✔ Contribute to planning in your own way by putting forward suggestions of your own, particularly if you support an individual pupil.

✔ Check that you understand plans if anything is not clear to you.

Don't

✗ Criticise plans – if you have suggestions make them sensitively.

✗ Try to change plans unless you have been asked to do so.

✗ Worry if pupils finish activities in advance – but have something else up your sleeve if they do!

Transport

Communication and language
- Describe a vehicle to children and ask them to identify it.
- Put your hand in the feely bag and describe the vehicle.
- Talking about different vehicles and why we have them.

Physical development
- Variety of ride-on vehicles in the outdoor area.
- Car wash for vehicles.
- Vehicles in the sand/diggers in gravel.
- Large tyres in outside area filled with different materials.
- Making vehicles out of dough.

Personal, social and emotional development
- Talk about journeys they have taken.
- Visit by road safety officer.
- Working co-operatively to build a vehicle using construction/junk materials.

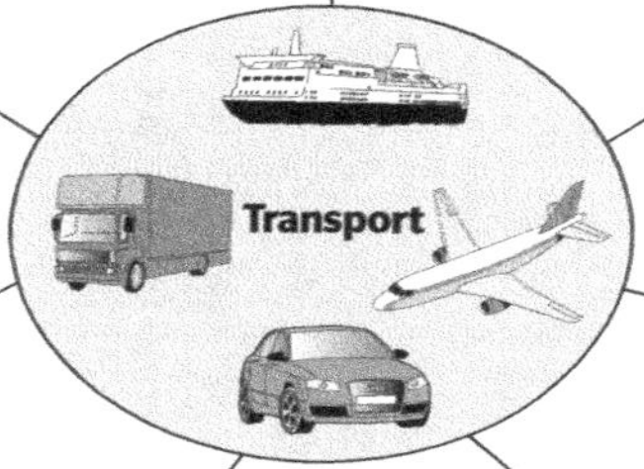

Expressive arts and design
- Make a vehicle of your own.
- Role play area – airport, inside a bus or car, a petrol station.
- Paint tracks using tyres of different sizes.
- Draw a vehicle using 'paint' on the computer.

Understanding the world
- Rolling vehicles down a ramp – which will go the furthest?
- Remote controlled cars/bee-bots to describe direction and use positional language.
- Find the road you live on using a simplified local map.
- Make a ferry for the water tray.

Literacy
- Any stories or books about transport.
- Transport songs and rhymes – Wheels on the bus, The big ship sails, Row, row your boat, 5 Little Men in a flying saucer, A sailor went to sea, This is the way we cross the road.
- Drawing letter shapes in the sand using cars.

Mathematics
- Ordering different vehicles by size.
- Sorting vehicles into colours, number of wheels.
- Problem solving – how many people can you fit on the bus?
- Picture graph showing types of transport children have used/how they get to school.

Figure 2.1 An example of a plan for Reception with the theme of Transport

Brilliant case study

Neil is an experienced teaching assistant who is working with a newly qualified or early career teacher (ECT) in Year 8. They have been working well throughout the autumn term and the teacher sends Neil her plans each week in advance. However, on looking through the maths plans for the following week, Neil has noticed that she is aiming to deliver an ambitious lesson to the group which he knows that some of the pupils he supports are going to struggle with.

- Should Neil say something and if so, what?
- How can this situation be managed sensitively if these kinds of issues continue?

Subject specialisms

As the role of the teaching assistant has developed, in some secondary schools there have also been developments in the way in which staff are allocated in different departments. If you have a particular strength in a subject you may be asked to stay within that subject area so that you can support teaching and learning more effectively. You will also be able to develop your own knowledge of the subject and work more closely on planning as there will be fewer time constraints. This has benefits for pupils as you will get to know the curriculum in your subject as well as the plans which are delivered by teachers.

Brilliant example

Sam works in the computing department of a secondary school. He is a graduate in computer science and has taken a teaching assistant job at the school as he is interested in pursuing a career as a teacher. He has been able to work closely with the department and has supported computing teachers in updating the school's website as well as supporting teaching and learning within the school.

You may also be asked to work in a specific curriculum area if this is dictated by the needs of the school. In this case you may need to develop your own subject knowledge. If you need to do this, a good starting point will be to think about your knowledge and skills in relation to the curriculum that you are supporting. You can do this in different ways:

- identify your knowledge of the curriculum area
- think about transferable skills which you may be able to bring to the subject
- speak to teachers about expectations within the curriculum area and sit in on lessons
- speak to or work alongside other teaching assistants who have supported the subject
- seek advice and support through your own continuing professional development

Brilliant case study

Ann has been asked to work within the biology department at her school as there are not enough support staff for this area. Although she has studied the subject at school herself this was a long time ago and she does not feel confident enough to support pupils in biology. She usually works in the geography and PE departments.

- What might be a good starting point for Ann?
- How could she use support available within the school and beyond to support her knowledge and skills?

In either case you will need to work with teachers to ensure that you contribute to planning, delivery and evaluation of lessons wherever possible. If you are employed by the school to support an individual pupil you will need to stay with them to assist with all curriculum subjects, depending on the amount of hours support they have.

Brilliant recap

- Be clear on the curriculum requirements for the age and stage of the pupils you are supporting.
- If you cannot see or talk about plans in advance, discuss other ways of finding out.
- Make sure you know learning objectives and finer details of the plan.
- Find out about how colleagues in other schools are involved in planning.
- Support the school curriculum using your own areas of expertise.

Further reading

www.gov.uk – National Curriculum

www.education.gov.scot/education-scotland – Scottish curriculum

www.nidirect.gov.uk – Northern Ireland Curriculum

www.gov.wales/current-school-curriculum-guide – Welsh curriculum

Chapter 3

Supporting teaching and learning – making an effective contribution

Supporting teaching and learning is a key aspect of your role, and the way in which you do this will make a huge difference to pupils, both academically and emotionally. In order to do this effectively as a teaching assistant you will need the support of the whole school team.

You may be asked to support individuals, groups or even whole classes depending on your experience, qualifications and knowledge. It is also likely that at some stage you will be asked to support pupil learning outside the classroom, for example on school visits, during outdoor activities or as part of extended school provision, such as clubs. In some cases you may need to support pupils during digital and online learning sessions. At all times you will need to encourage independent learning through being an enabler to pupils and to support their understanding – remember you are not there to carry out the task for them! If you need to give pupils too much support, they are not able to manage the task and you should refer to the class or subject teacher.

When you start in a new role you should always find out if you will be expected to cover whole classes – policies vary between schools, academy trusts and local authorities but in most cases you should not be asked to do this unless you are an HLTA or have been specifically trained as a cover supervisor. You will need to work with teachers to ensure that you have a good understanding of what you are expected to do and make sure that you are working towards clear learning objectives and that pupils are also aware of them. Even from the earliest stages it is useful to talk to pupils about what they are trying to find out and why they are working on a particular task or in a particular way.

Planning

Although you may not have time to plan with teachers individually – although some assistants do – you should try to find out in advance what you will be expected to work on with pupils. Depending on the relationship you have with teachers and how regularly you are able to speak to them, this may be a challenge due to time constraints. If at all possible, you should ask to see a lesson plan so that you are best prepared to support pupils – in some classrooms you will find that plans are displayed on the wall, or they may be accessible online, for example on the school intranet or saved in a Microsoft Teams or SharePoint folder. If you are unable to see plans it is important that you find out before a lesson:

- the learning objective (or what pupils are expected to be able to do at the end of the lesson). This is sometimes known as the WALT (we are learning to) or just the LO (learning objective)
- who you are going to be working with
- any resources that you are expected to use and how to use them

If you do not have this information before walking into the class, it will mean that you are not making full use of your time as a support to both teacher and pupils.

(For more on planning see Chapter 2.)

Brilliant tip

Make it part of your routine with pupils to write down the learning objective as a heading before starting to work on an activity. This will reinforce what they are being asked to do and bring the learning objective forward in everyone's mind. You will also be able to refer pupils back to it quickly.

Research into the impact of teaching assistants in schools

A project to maximise the impact of teaching assistants in schools followed research in the area of classroom support by a large scale study, the Deployment and Impact of Support Staff (DISS) between 2003 and 2009. The study was wide ranging and looked at support staff in all types of schools and all pupils and involved 18,000 responses from school staff. Its findings were around academic progress in English, maths and science (*Maximising the Impact of Teaching Assistants* by Rob Webster, Anthony Russell and Peter Blatchford (Routledge 2016)). The study showed that many teachers had not been trained in how to work effectively with teaching assistants and that the way in which they were managed varied widely. The project looking at the Effective Deployment of Teaching Assistants (EDTA) led to the MITA programme (Maximising the Impact of Teaching Assistants), which has now become a training programme for schools.

After extensive work in this area, it was clear that the responsibility for the impact of teaching assistants lies with the way in which they are used or deployed in schools, and the project produced a series of recommendations:

- schools should assess and potentially re-evaluate the way in which TAs are deployed
- effective interactions between TAs and pupils are key to the TA role
- TA and teacher training and collaboration is vital to support pupil achievement

Whilst the level of training and the way in which you are deployed in your school will not be in your control, you can think about and evaluate the way in which you interact with pupils when supporting their learning.

How to use talk effectively with pupils

One of the MITA programme findings was about the importance of interacting effectively when supporting pupils' learning. This involves thinking carefully about how you approach your conversations with pupils to ensure that they achieve the best outcomes during the session. Remember we are trying to find out what pupils know as well as ensuring that they work as independently as possible.

Brilliant example

Example 1. Adult: Who were the UK at war with in World War 2?

Pupil: Poland

Adult: No, the UK was at war with Germany.

Example 2. Adult: What can you tell me about World War 2?

Pupil: We were at war and bombs were dropped on our cities, people had to sleep in shelters or underground, and some children were sent away from cities to keep them safe.

Adult: Yes, well done. How would you feel about being sent away from home? What other differences might there have been from your life today?

In the first example, the adult has asked a question which limits the possibility of further extending the pupil's knowledge. In the second case, the question is more open and invites the pupil to talk about what they know. This gives the adult the opportunity to develop their existing knowledge and question them further.

The study explores different types of talk with pupils, and the importance of using more open questioning so that further questions can build on what pupils know. Before framing questions with pupils, think about the kind of answer you would like to have and how you can build on it. This takes time and skill, but is more likely to promote a discussion and a shared learning experience for pupils.

Brilliant activity

The next time you watch an experienced teacher or TA, note down the kinds of questions they are asking pupils and how they find out about what they are thinking. Then consider how they use these to build on pupils' knowledge.

Understanding the use of scaffolding

The term 'scaffolding' may not be familiar to you, but as a teaching assistant it is one of the tools which is available to you when supporting children during learning activities. This is because a teaching assistant is more likely to be based close to an individual or group and so can do this more quickly when the pupil is working on a task.

Scaffolding is the process by which we support pupils towards meeting learning objectives by assessing their progress and giving them some kind of immediate verbal feedback when needed, although this should be after they have had time to try and work towards the objective independently and should be based on their responses. We should also be giving them strategies to manage their learning when they are 'stuck'. In addition, by talking to them about the importance of facing challenges and of making mistakes and learning from them, we are showing pupils that this is part of the process.

Through scaffolding, pupils can be encouraged to think about the steps or strategies that they are using. Along with the use of praise and effective questioning, this will develop pupils' confidence and reassure them during learning activities.

Brilliant case study

Rosanna is working with a group of children on some long division problems. One of the group, Mikey, is telling her that he can't do it and doesn't understand it as there are too many things to remember.

- What could Rosanna say to Mikey?
- How might the use of scaffolding help in this situation?
- Why will this also benefit Mikey in the future?

Using praise

Whenever you are supporting teaching and learning, and at whatever age, you should not underestimate the power of praise. Pupils will always respond positively to encouragement and recognition for the task they are undertaking. It is likely that you will do this anyway without thinking about it, but it is important to be aware of its impact on pupil learning: verbal praise in particular can be very powerful. The school might also have a system for giving out stickers, stamps or team points to pupils for effort and achievement, depending on their age. However, you should check which of these are used where you are working as you will need to make sure that you follow school policy.

Brilliant case study

Jamal is supporting in Year 1 and has recently started working in a new school. He is an experienced assistant and has always kept stickers in his pocket to hand out to pupils. During maths he notices that one girl is trying particularly hard and gives her a sticker. Later on, the class teacher tells Jamal that stickers are never used in that particular school and that verbal praise is seen as far more powerful. Jamal is very surprised.

- What do you think about Jamal's reaction?
- Is anyone in the wrong here?
- What else could Jamal do the next time he sees the girl trying hard?

Factors which will affect pupil learning

You may well find that whilst you are working with pupils you regularly come up against difficulties – this is bound to happen and will affect the most experienced practitioners! The kinds of problems you may face will vary and the more experienced you become it is likely that you will see them coming – sometimes before they have happened – and are able to avoid them. The important thing is to remember that your response will make a difference to how this resolves itself – or doesn't.

Problems you may encounter include the following.

Ability and creativity

Pupils will always have different levels of ability and will have skills in different areas. They may also feel that they are not able to achieve in a particular area, for example in writing or maths, or in more creative subjects such as art or music. This may affect their motivation and what they are able to do. You should always try to encourage them to try new things and to take risks with their learning.

Age and maturity

Pupils will develop at their own pace and learning will occur at different rates in different children even though there will be an average age at which children achieve various milestones. Remember also that in any one class there will be a spread of ages, in other words, the oldest in the year group will be born in September whilst others may not have their birthdays until the end of the academic year. At the earliest stages of schooling this may well make quite a difference and it may be worth finding out about children's birthdays, particularly when working on assessments, and to look at whether the results are age-adjusted.

Gender

Some pupils may come from a background which has given them more or fewer learning opportunities due to their gender. For example, a boy might be given more academic encouragement than his sister due to family expectations. As school staff it is important that we do not discriminate due to gender, for example by only allowing girls to do cooking activities, or only boys to do football. We should also consider the needs of gender-neutral pupils or those who are hoping to transition (see also Chapter 7).

Physical factors

There are a number of reasons that physical factors might affect learning. Depending on their age and maturity, some pupils may have less control over their fine and gross motor skills, which might impact on their ability to carry out a task. Fine motor skills are skills such as holding a pencil or using a knife and fork effectively, while gross motor skills are skills such as running, jumping, skipping and whole body movements. Also if pupils have additional needs such as a visual impairment, this might mean that they need more support in order to access the curriculum.

Ability to remain on task

Pupils of different ages will vary in their ability to concentrate on a task – broadly speaking, the younger the child, the shorter the concentration span. They may also look for more reassurance from adults and those around them. As pupils become older, most will be able to concentrate for a set time without becoming distracted. At any stage, if one or a group of pupils' ability to concentrate is very different from that of their classmates, this may affect the learning of others.

Pupils' ability to remain on task will also be influenced by any specific learning needs they may have. These may be for example conditions such as ADD (Attention Deficit Disorder). If you have concerns about a pupil you should speak to a teacher or your school's SENDCo.

Linguistic factors

Language is the key element to pupil learning. If pupils have problems such as a speech and language disorder or have not been encouraged to socialise with others, they may find learning more challenging. This is because language is the route through which we begin to learn to rationalise our thoughts in an abstract way. We need to encourage the development of language as much as possible in children from the earliest stage so that they are given as much opportunity as possible to develop their confidence and vocabulary.

As well as speaking to pupils as much as possible during learning activities we must also encourage discussion and a wide range of stories and first-hand experiences. Pupils who speak English as an additional language can also find it harder to learn if they are not supported effectively (see Chapter 7). In more extreme cases, those who have limited language may also have behavioural difficulties if they are unable to vocalise their feelings, which can in turn lead to frustration.

Emotional factors

Pupils will naturally be affected by their home background and whether this is happy and settled. There can be a huge number of reasons why this is not the case at any one time and it is likely to depend on a wide number of issues, such as bereavement, separated parents or new parental partners, alcoholism in the family and so on. Pupils may also become upset about things which may seem insignificant to an adult, such as being unable to say goodbye to a parent that day or an argument with a friend or sibling. In cases like this you may need to remove the pupil and speak to them about what is upsetting them so that you are able to continue. If they are too upset to work you will be unable to make them do so.

Social, cultural and ethnic background

All pupils will be affected by their background and whether they have had positive social experiences. This will affect their learning, for example if they have had limited experience of meeting others, which may in turn give them less confidence. In areas of social deprivation you may find that pupils have come to school without eating or without enough clothes. These kinds of issues will also affect their ability to learn. Depending on pupils' culture or ethnicity they may have learned to do things in a particular way which may not be in keeping with that of the school. Remember, if you have reason to be concerned about a pupil you should refer this to a member of teaching staff.

Motivation

We all know what it feels like to be motivated by something and pupils will be no different. Motivation will clearly affect their learning as it is the interest they have in a task. If a pupil does not see a purpose to what they are doing, the task is unclear or they are unable to do it, they will quickly become demotivated. It is important that any adults working with the child ensure that they are able to carry out the task and that it makes sense to them.

Problems with resources

You should make sure in advance that you have sufficient resources, particularly if they are slightly different from the usual. Even if the teacher has set these up for you it is still worth checking to make sure you have enough of everything. If you are working with pupils who have additional needs you will need to make sure that all the resources are appropriate for them and that they will be able to access the curriculum as much as the other pupils. Remember, if you are working with technology such as computers, you should always have alternative plans if for some reason they don't work!

Environmental factors

Depending on the environment, you may find that the area you are working in has been booked by someone else, there is insufficient space for the number of pupils, or is too hot, too cold or too noisy. Always check the area first if at all possible. If you have been unable to do this beforehand and it is unsuitable you will need to find an alternative to ensure that the pupils are able to benefit from the activity. There is no point in attempting to work there if, for example, there is a lot of noise immediately outside the room, or if the temperature in the room is not conducive to learning.

Brilliant activity

Although this will not be possible for all, consider which of these problems you should be able to avoid by planning ahead, before starting to carry out tasks with pupils.

Supporting individuals

There may be a number of reasons you are supporting an individual pupil. The first is that you have been specifically employed to support them in the classroom because they have an Education and Health Care Plan (EHCP) with specific targets. However, you may also work periodically with pupils who have specific learning needs such as dyslexia if you support different classes or are based in learning support. If you are working with an individual pupil you should make sure you know something about them before you start – even if this is something about their interests or talents. This will be invaluable to you whilst you are supporting teaching and learning. This is because it may help you to draw them out and develop a relationship with them.

If you are employed to directly work one to one with a pupil you will also need to find out as much as you can about their needs and individual educational targets on paperwork such as EHCPs, Individual Education Plans (IEPS) and Personal Support Plans (PSPs). You should speak to your school's SENDCo or inclusion manager to clarify how you should work on specific targets and how much time you will need to work alone with them, or whether you should support them as part of a group. Remember to always speak to teachers if you are not clear about your role when supporting individual pupils.

You may also be asked to work with more able pupils, although in many cases their work will be differentiated as they may be set different challenges from other pupils.

Supporting groups

Most teaching assistants will work with groups on a regular basis. This may be as part of an intervention programme within the school which you are involved with or simply as part of your work within the classroom. If you have been asked to work with a group, it may sound obvious but you should remember to involve all pupils – it is easy to just focus your questioning on those who are eager to answer. Quieter pupils will often benefit from working in small groups as it will help their confidence, so try to draw them in wherever possible. Look out for those who are losing concentration as they may start to distract others or gain attention in a negative way. You may also have been given a group who do not work well together – do not be afraid of speaking to the teacher about it if the group does not 'gel'. (For more on involving and engaging with all pupils, see Chapter 7.)

Intervention groups

Many teaching assistants now work with pupils in what are known as intervention groups. These groups will usually focus on a specific area of additional support which the pupils need, most commonly in English and maths, and will take place outside the classroom. They may be based on programmes of learning which are commercially available or teachers may give you specific plans to work with based on the needs of the pupils you are supporting.

Brilliant case study

Andre has been asked to work with a group of six Year 7 pupils on a regular basis to focus on developing their basic maths skills. He has been given a list of the skills that they need to work on but has not had any more information from the maths teacher.

- What further information should Andre be given?
- Why is it important that Andre is given appropriate support when working with this group?

Supporting whole classes

You may be asked to cover whole classes as part of your role in a mainstream school. If you have had specific training or are very experienced you may be equipped to do this. However, you should make sure that you are covered by insurance (you should not take PE lessons, for example, unless you have specific training) and know what you are expected to cover, as teachers should plan for you.

Teaching assistants are also sometimes asked to cover for Planning, Preparation and Assessment (PPA) time for teachers, and this has been the subject of discussion in the educational press and in online social media groups.

There is no legal reason why you should not take whole classes as some teaching assistants are very experienced and qualified. However, if you are uncomfortable or do not feel experienced enough to do it you should say so. If you are unhappy with what you are being asked to do you should check your contract and job description to see whether it includes any mention of cover supervision under your duties.

Cover supervision

Cover supervisors are most often found in secondary schools but can also be found in primary and special schools. They may be asked to take lessons on a regular basis and cover for staff absence although they should not be asked to plan lessons themselves. If you are a cover supervisor you should have advance warning that you are going to take a class so that you are able to discuss plans with teachers, or at least be left detailed plans. You should not be asked to plan and mark work for teachers.

Brilliant tip

When working with groups or whole classes, agree ground rules with them during your first session and talk to them about what will happen if these are not met. This will make it clear what is acceptable to the group and what is not. It is far easier to manage pupils if they are aware of the boundaries and agree rules together. You should always make sure that these are phrased positively; for example 'always show respect to others' rather than focusing on the negative of 'don't do this', as this is a more positive use of language. It will also make expectations clear.

Monitoring and modifying activities whilst you are working with pupils

It is likely that at some stage you will need to modify or change the work that pupils are carrying out with you – this is completely normal, but you need to be ready for it. An example might be if you are working with a group and some pupils finish their work before others: you may need to give them additional work to do (often called an extension activity). You should check with the teacher whether you need to do this and if they have something in mind *before* you start working with the group. It is also possible that a pupil is working much faster or much slower than the rest of the group. In this situation you should speak to the pupil and ask them to check their work before moving on to the next activity.

When to refer to others

You may find that while you are working with pupils you need to refer back to the teacher. This could be for a number of reasons, although you should make sure that you have done what you can first. You will need to be sensitive when doing this, for example do not try to speak to the teacher when they are busy or occupied with other pupils – make sure you choose your moment carefully!

Reasons may include:

- pupil behaviour
- activity is too hard or too easy for pupils
- a pupil who has special educational needs is unable to access the task

If you are unable to speak to the teacher for the time being, make sure you give pupils an alternative activity or in cases of poor behaviour, separate them from one another in the meantime.

Brilliant dos and don'ts

Do

- ✔ Do make sure you are ready and fully prepared each time you support pupils.
- ✔ Do make sure you have seen plans and know the learning objectives.
- ✔ Do use your initiative if you spot something that needs doing.
- ✔ Do make sure you feed back to the teacher afterwards, even if this is through handwritten notes and feedback sheets.

Don't

- ✗ Don't call across the class to the teacher, particularly if they are busy with pupils.
- ✗ Don't interrupt the flow of the lesson by adding your own comments when the teacher is speaking to the class.
- ✗ Don't forget that your own voice can be a distraction when the teacher is talking. Keep it down as much as possible.
- ✗ Don't 'over prompt' pupils – direct their learning through questioning to extend their thinking.

Carrying out pupil assessments and observations

You should be carrying out assessments on pupils all the time as part of the work you do in supporting teaching and learning in schools. Teachers have to monitor and assess pupil achievement throughout the academic year and your role is to support them in doing this so that they can feed back to headteachers. Assessment may take different forms:

Formative assessment

This is everyday assessment, which takes place through observations, questioning and talking to pupils to check their understanding. You should always monitor what pupils say to you whilst carrying out learning activities as this will enable you to do this.

Summative assessment

This is used to check learning at the end of a topic, year or scheme of work so that teachers can recap and assess how much pupils have achieved. It could be that this takes the form of SATS or end of year tests prior to writing school reports.

Assessment for learning

This is increasingly used by schools to monitor pupil learning using peer- and self-assessment. Assessment for learning is a way in which pupils are asked to take more responsibility for their own learning. Through it, pupils are able to understand the aim of what they are doing, what they need to do to reach that aim and where they are in relation to it through measuring their own progress. You may be asked to support them in doing this by clarifying pupils' understanding of learning objectives and making sure that they are on track with their learning. They can also be encouraged to peer assess and to build up their techniques through working with adults and their peers so that they will be able to look more objectively at their own achievements. Assessment for learning also supports the encouragement of high expectation by emphasising the achievement of pupils rather than focusing on what they can't do. Many schools are adopting assessment for learning for use in all age groups so that pupils can develop self-assessment skills and can reflect on and recognise their own achievements, although it may look different in different year groups:

- In Reception and key stage 1, pupils may be asked to self-assess after a session using thumbs up or thumbs down, or a traffic light or emoji.
- In key stage 2, pupils may be asked to colour code their work to show their level of understanding. They may also start to peer-assess one another's work.
- In secondary schools, pupils may discuss their own progress as a whole class or group plenary at the end of the session.

When supporting assessment for learning, you will need to use different techniques and be aware of how they can enhance what pupils are doing, as well as knowing when you should refer to others (see Figure 3.1).

Brilliant tip

If your school uses assessment for learning or AfL, ask whether you can observe it in progress. If there is whole school training on AfL, support staff should also be able to attend.

Benefits for teachers

Effective assessment for learning will enable the teacher to pass on the responsibility to the child over time for managing their own learning so that they will become more actively involved in the process.

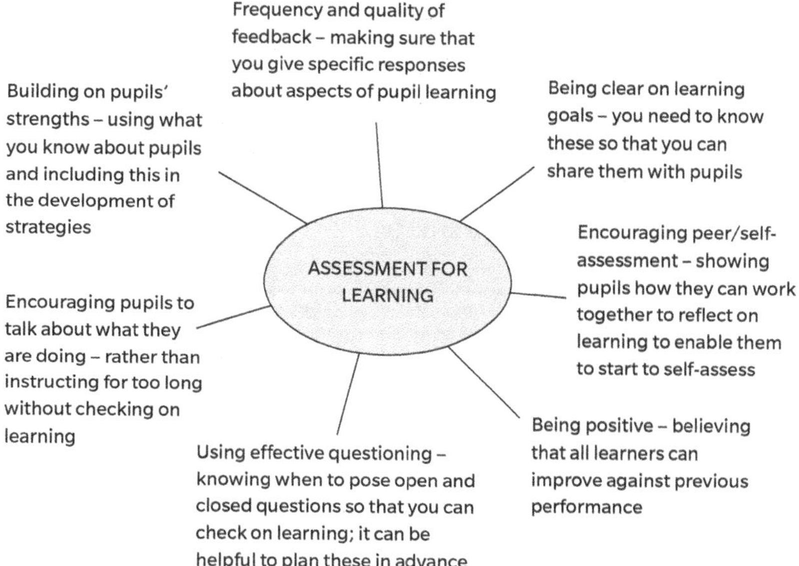

Figure 3.1 Strategies for supporting assessment for learning

Benefits for pupils

The process will inform pupils about how they approach learning and tackle areas on which they need to work. They will be able to consider areas for improvement by looking at assessment criteria and develop their ability to self-assess. Their increased awareness of how to learn will develop their confidence and help them to recognise when to ask for support.

Benefits for you

Assessment for learning will inform how you approach pupil questioning based on what you have discovered about how they learn. You may need to pace the progress of learners depending on their needs, so that less able pupils are given opportunities to revisit areas of uncertainty.

At the start of any activity, pupils need to be clear about what they are going to learn and how they will be assessed. For assessment for learning to be effective, pupils need to know what they are learning, why they are learning it and how the assessment will take place. If you are able to work on this with pupils they should be able to think about their learning after each activity and consider how their learning in the future may be affected.

Brilliant activity

The next time you are working with a group of pupils, make sure you clarify the learning objectives and assessment criteria with them and encourage them to continue to check their learning against these throughout the session, either alone or with a partner. Consider how much careful management of pupil learning encourages them to achieve at a higher level.

Observations

Although you will be observing pupils all the time, you may be asked to carry out observations without working directly with a pupil for a specific reason, which may be:

- to observe how the pupil interacts with others
- to look at the way in which a pupil approaches their learning
- to observe as part of the early years foundation stage
- to monitor a pupil's special educational need
- to monitor behaviour

When carrying out observations, check with the teacher how you should record the information, whether there is a specific format and how much detail is required. For example, you may only need to complete a checklist to note down how often something specific happens, rather than writing everything down, in which case you should be given a template. Your observation may also be timed, so you may only need to spend a few minutes on it. Make sure you know what you are looking for and only record what you can see.

Brilliant case study

Andi has been asked to observe a Year 3 child on the playground and has been told that staff have raised concerns about him. However Andi is not clear on exactly what she is looking for or how to record it.

- Why is it important that Andi is clear on the purpose of the observation?
- What kind of information would be helpful for Andi?

Providing feedback to teachers

Although everyone in schools always seems to be extremely busy, you should make sure that you always give feedback to teachers about your work with pupils. Some teachers and teaching assistants do this as a matter of course, but in some schools it is harder than others to find time, and secondary school staff in particular can find it very difficult due to the way in which the curriculum and timetable is structured. Although it can be quicker to give verbal feedback to teachers this can sometimes be 'lost' in the course of a busy day. Some assistants might jot down notes and give them to teachers at the end of the session, particularly if the pupil or pupils with whom they are working have found the task very difficult or too easy. It is sometimes also helpful to write down specific phrases or vocabulary which a pupil has used. In some schools it is the policy to complete more formal feedback sheets which will give a clear breakdown of each pupil's response whilst in others, teachers may ask you to mark pupils' work and leave comments such as 'Supported by TA' with a breakdown of how pupils managed the task (an example of a feedback form is given in Appendix 2). In other cases, assistants may email or contact teachers at the end of the day with annotated plans or other methods of feedback so that they have it before the next day.

The use of technologies, digital and online learning

Whether or not you are confident when using technology, it is likely that you will need to know at least some of the basics so that you can support pupils more effectively. You may be lucky enough to receive training in this, but in many cases teaching assistants will be learning 'on the job'. The types of technology you are likely to use will include interactive whiteboards, laptops, tablets and PCs, and you may be asked to set these up in preparation for lessons as well as use them as part of the classes you support. In addition, routine tasks such as taking registers are now increasingly likely to be carried out using a computer. Teaching assistants who work with pupils who have special educational needs and disabilities may also use specific technological resources to support pupils, for example communication aids such as Voice Output Communication Aids (VOCAs), which can produce the sound of a voice. (For more on supporting pupils who have special educational needs and disabilities, see Chapter 6.)

As well as these technologies, since the pandemic in 2020 many teachers now also use digital learning platforms so that pupils can access lessons from home. If you are confident in using technology, you may be asked to support this by planning and setting up classes or working alongside teachers to do this; however, you are likely to be given training in this instance to help you.

There are also many more resources available online to support teaching and learning for teachers and teaching assistants, as well as social media groups and blogs so that those who are working in schools can share and compare ideas. (Some examples of these are provided below, although they are likely to be changing and evolving all the time.)

Brilliant recap

- Be prepared for all eventualities!
- Remember the importance of planning and feedback.
- Use effective questioning and dialogue to support pupils' learning.
- Encourage pupils to reflect on their own progress and use assessment for learning.
- Be aware that you are observing and assessing pupils at all times.
- Remember the power of praise.

Further reading

Webster, Rob, Russell, Anthony and Blatchford, Peter (2016) *Maximising the Impact of Teaching Assistants*, Routledge.

Bosanquet, Paula, Radford, Julie and Webster, Rob (2016) *The Teaching Assistant's Guide to Effective Interaction – How to Maximise your Practice*, Routledge.

Gershon, Mike (2013) *How to use Assessment for Learning in the Classroom: The Complete Guide*, CreateSpace Independent Publishing Platform.

Online resources

www.primaryresources.co.uk/ – a range of lesson plans and other resources

Teaching Assistant Hub: https://universityprimaryschool.org.uk/research-development/press-articles-and-book/ (also on Twitter@UKTAHUB) – an initiative for TAs to share strategies

TWINKL and Pinterest have a separate area for teaching assistants:

www.twinkl.co.uk/resources/teaching-assistants

www.pinterest.co.uk/twinklta/

Free courses for TAs: www.open.edu/openlearn/education-development/resources-teaching-assistants

Wellbeing support for TAs:

www.educationsupport.org.uk/resources/for-individuals/guides/wellbeing-resources-for-teaching-assistants/

Social media platforms also have specific groups for teaching assistants if you search by 'teaching assistants'.

Chapter 4

Safeguarding and pastoral care of pupils

As a teaching assistant, you are likely to develop relationships with pupils and find that they trust you and confide in you. Alternatively, in some cases, pupils may not want to talk about what is happening in their lives and adults will need to look out for signs that something is wrong. In both cases, if a child confides in you or you have any particular concerns about their welfare, you will need to speak to others. In this chapter we will look at your responsibilities around safeguarding as well as those of others in the school, and who you should inform.

Closely linked to the area of safeguarding is providing pastoral support and care to pupils, and this will also be part of your role as a teaching assistant. Generally speaking, pastoral support means looking after pupils' physical, social or emotional needs. You may be the adult whom pupils will approach with any issues or problems which they may feel that they are not able to talk about with others. You may also be asked to support different stages in pupils' education by supporting teachers as they prepare pupils for different transitions, as well as working with pupils on citizenship and local community projects.

Teaching assistants may also deal with situations which arise on a regular basis, such as mentoring and supporting pupils' mental health, and also using restorative justice, which is becoming widely used in schools for resolving conflict situations (for more on restorative justice, see Chapter 5).

Safeguarding

All adults in schools have a responsibility to safeguard children and young people from harm and to look after their welfare. As professionals we have a duty to ensure that children and young people are protected as much as possible.

You may hear different terms used to describe the way in which we do this. While the term 'child protection' refers to the way in which we respond to harm in relation to children, 'safeguarding' means the steps we take to prevent it from happening.

Legislation and guidance

There are two key government documents which you will need to be aware of in the context of safeguarding. Both documents are regularly updated so you should check for the most up to date versions:

- Keeping Children Safe in Education (DfE, 2023): Statutory Guidance for Schools and Colleges: This document sets out how practitioners should fulfil their safeguarding obligations. All staff should read Part One of this guidance.
- Working together to Safeguard Children (HM Government, 2023): This document is a guide to how practitioners and other agencies should work together to help, protect and promote the welfare of children.

As stated in the first document, it is a legal requirement for schools to have a safeguarding policy and a member of staff who is responsible for keeping children safe, who is known as the Designated Safeguarding Lead (DSL). You will need to be aware of both and be clear on the requirements of the policy. Included in the school safeguarding policy should be:

- staff recruitment – to ensure that potential staff have had criminal record checks before working with pupils
- staff/volunteer training and code of conduct
- how and when to report safeguarding concerns
- prevention of bullying
- e-safety and security when online

Schools will need to provide advice and ensure that children and young people are safe when they are online. It is important to develop their awareness that it is not always safe to talk to other people, especially those that they do not know. They should be encouraged to talk to an adult if they have any concerns or worries or if they are asked to do something they do not feel comfortable with. Schools may also run information evenings for parents and carers to give them advice and support about internet safety and highlight potential problems.

Brilliant activity

Find a copy of your school's safeguarding policy. What measures does the school have in place for monitoring safeguarding? How do they ensure that pupils can access only safe websites when online in school?

The second document gives information and advice about working with others with regard to safeguarding. Your local authority will have a local safeguarding partnership or LSP, which has been set up to promote and co-ordinate the safeguarding and welfare of children in your area. If your school does have a concern, the local authority will also act alongside it to follow guidelines and ensure that all agencies work together. The kinds of issues which may arise in schools will vary – however, you should always be alert to any safeguarding concerns and ensure that you are acting appropriately and within the correct guidelines.

Brilliant tip

Find out what you can about your local LSP and the support they offer for:

- children and young people
- schools
- parents and carers

In addition to these documents, if you are working in the early years foundation stage, you should have read Section 3 of the EYFS Statutory Framework, which outlines the safeguarding and welfare requirements in the early years. These include staff suitability, adult–child ratios, support and training with regard to safeguarding.

Brilliant case study

Pushra works as a teaching assistant in the Reception class in a small primary school. She is completing an early years qualification and as part of the course is looking at effective safeguarding practice. She realises that the school have not given her any information or training on safeguarding since she started in her role.

- Describe what Pushra should do.
- Why is it important that she takes some action?

Types and possible signs of abuse

You should always be alert to any signs that a pupil is the victim of abuse – these signs might include both physical and behavioural changes. There are four main types of abuse.

Physical

This involves being physically hurt or injured. Children and young people may suffer physical abuse from an adult on a persistent or spasmodic basis. If you notice any frequent signs of injury such as regular bruises, burns or cuts, or repeated absences without a satisfactory explanation, it is important to take further action by speaking to your DSL. Less obvious signs of physical abuse may include fear of physical contact with others, reluctance to get changed for PE or sports sessions, or wanting to stay covered up, even in hot weather.

Emotional

Emotional abuse which is carried out by adults can involve the pupil continuously being 'put down' and criticised, as well as name calling, humiliation or bullying. Over time this will affect their emotional development.

Signs of emotional abuse are that a pupil may become withdrawn or lack confidence, show regression or be 'clingy' towards adults, and have low self-esteem. Pupils who suffer from emotional abuse are more likely to be anxious about new situations and may appear distracted and unable to concentrate.

Sexual

This involves an adult or young person abusing a child sexually, for example by touching their bodies inappropriately or by forcing them to look at sexual images or have sex. Signs to look out for may include sexual behaviour which is inappropriate to the child's age, genital irritation, clinginess or changes in the pupil's behaviour, appearing withdrawn or lacking trust in adults. Sexual abuse can be very difficult to identify and its signs may also indicate other kinds of abuse. Child Sexual Exploitation (CSE) is another form of sexual abuse.

Neglect

This type of abuse means that the child or young person is not having their basic needs met by parents or carers. These basic needs include shelter, food, general hygiene, love and medical care. The signs of neglect may be that pupils are dirty, hungry, attention seeking or generally failing to thrive.

In addition to these four forms of abuse, domestic abuse is often classified as a form of child abuse.

It occurs when there is violence, bullying, threatening behaviour or coercive control within a household which is witnessed by a child or young person. The effects can include changes in behaviour such as aggression or antisocial behaviour as well as withdrawal, anxiety and eating disorders, although there may be other signs.

Online abuse and grooming

Although the types of abuse above may be caused by the child or young person's parent or carer, other types of abuse may be inflicted by their peers or by adults in a position of trust. One type of abuse which has become prevalent with the increased use of smartphones and social media is online abuse and cyber-bullying. This can be devastating and schools are increasingly speaking to children and young people and their parents and carers about being vigilant when going online. Bullying is just one aspect of online abuse – you should also be aware of the following:

Grooming

Grooming is the building of a relationship with a person to enable them to be manipulated or exploited. It can take place over a long or a short period of time and will usually lead to other forms of abuse such as sexual abuse, exploitation or radicalisation. Grooming may be carried out by peers or an adult and take place through different mediums, such as social media, texts or emails as well as through giving children and young people attention and gifts, and making them feel important. In older pupils, grooming may be carried out through forming romantic relationships.

Radicalisation

This form of abuse relates to coercing an individual or group of individuals into a set of extreme religious, political or social views. While older pupils are more likely to be radicalised than younger ones, it is also possible for parents and carers to become radicalised, which will affect the children or young people in their care. The government has produced a guidance document known as the Prevent Strategy, which is a counter-terrorism strategy to reduce the threat of terrorism in the UK. It emphasises the need for professionals such as social workers, the police, LSPs and Youth Offending Teams to work in partnership with one another. As part of the Prevent strategy, schools are also required to promote British values as part of a broad and balanced curriculum.

These values are:

1) respect for the rule of law
2) individual liberty
3) democracy
4) mutual respect
5) tolerance of different faiths and beliefs

Brilliant activity

Research British values and the reasons why schools are required to promote them.

Child Criminal Exploitation (CCE)

CCE is a form of grooming which usually takes place through gangs and puts pressure on children and young people to commit crimes. One of the most well-known forms of CCE is County Lines, in which young people are coerced into moving drugs from cities into smaller areas. They may be blackmailed or forced to do this once they have become involved with the gang and are likely to become dependent on drugs themselves.

Child Sexual Exploitation (CSE)

This form of abuse takes place when a child or young person believes that they are in a genuine romantic relationship and are given gifts, drugs or money in exchange for sexual activities. It is unlikely that they will know that they are being abused in this way and over time this abuse may change so that they are abused by more than one person, or are trafficked into different areas. CSE can happen in person or online, and victims may be asked to send explicit photos, which can then be used as blackmail.

Brilliant activity

Looking at the different forms of abuse, research and find out more about those you are less familiar with.

As a teaching assistant you are well placed to notice changes in pupils' behaviour or other possible signs of abuse. If a child confides in you about any form of abuse, you should always listen to what they tell you and report it to your DSL. If you are at all concerned, make sure you speak to your school's Designated Safeguarding Lead straightaway. They will follow school policy and if necessary report to the local authority. Always keep a note of what happened or what the pupil said, what you reported and who you told.

Risk factors for abuse

Risk factors mean that a child or young person may be more likely to be a victim of abuse, as they are likely to be more vulnerable.

These may include any or some of those factors listed in Figure 4.1, although you should be aware that their presence does not always mean that a pupil is at risk:

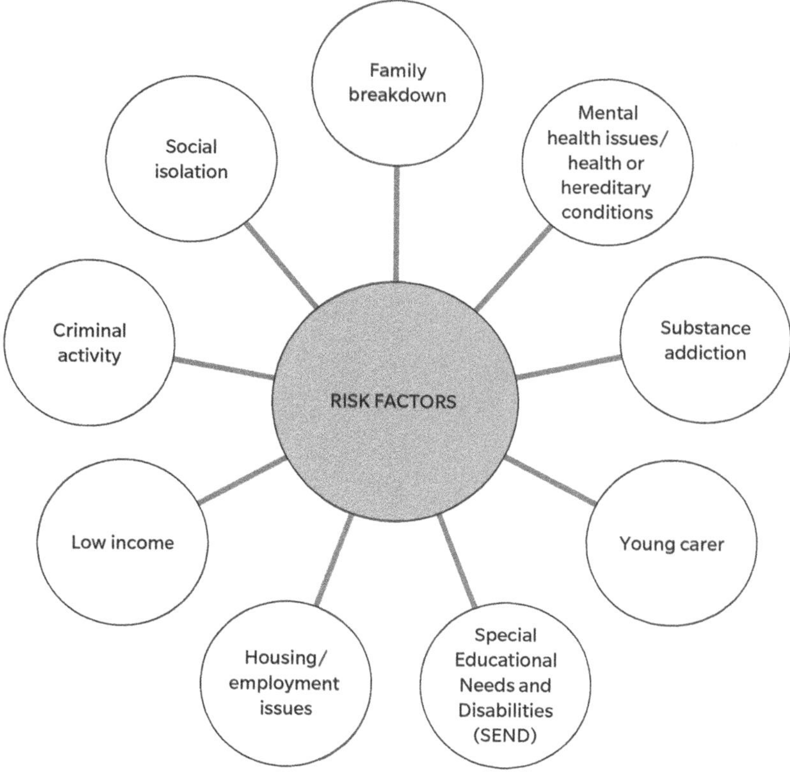

Figure 4.1 Risk factors

You may be working with pupils who have been identified as being at greater risk or on the 'at risk' register due to their current circumstances, for example those listed in Figure 4.1. Your role will be to support the pupil in a way which is defined by the school and by other professionals working with the child. These pupils should be supported by the school and outside agencies where appropriate and have a child protection plan in place to keep the child safe from harm. (In England, this is known as the child protection plan or CPP. In Wales, Scotland and Northern Ireland it is known as the child protection register or CPR). All agencies working with the pupil will need to be child centred, for example involving the pupil in meetings and asking for their opinion when discussing matters relating to them as much as possible. Information should only be shared on a need to know basis and should remain confidential and limited to those who need to know.

Brilliant tip

If you are going for an interview for a teaching assistant post, it is highly likely that you will be asked a question on safeguarding. Make sure you are up to date with current legislation and guidance and have looked at the school's policy.

Safe working

When you are with pupils in school in any context, and particularly if you are on your own, you should also think about your own working practice so that both you and pupils are protected. The kinds of issues you should think about are shown in Figure 4.2.

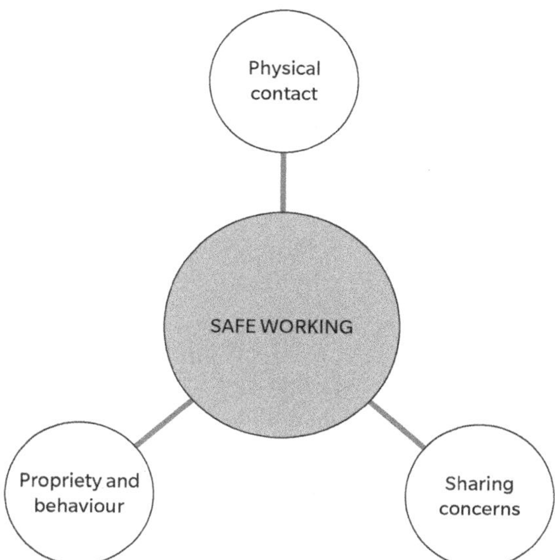

Figure 4.2 Safe working

Physical contact

You may rightly have concerns about any physical contact with children or young people; however, in some situations it is appropriate to put an arm around a child, for example if they are distressed or have hurt themselves. Young children can also often be demonstrative and will hug adults spontaneously. As a general rule, you should always act sensibly and behave reactively rather than initiating any physical contact with pupils, and in particular ensure that you do not have any physical contact with pupils if there is nobody else around. There are some situations in which this is not possible, for example if you are working with a pupil who has special educational needs and disabilities and you need to attend to their personal care. You must make sure that you follow school policy at all times when doing this, and if you are asked to do something you are not comfortable with for any reason you should speak to your DSL.

Brilliant tip

If you are in any doubt about whether or not you should have any physical contact with a pupil, it is always better not to.

Sharing concerns

You must always report any concerns to your school's Designated Safeguarding Lead (DSL) – whether this is based on what a pupil has said or because you have observed something – and record what has happened. In this way you will also be protected if any further incidents occur. You should also follow your school's whistleblowing policy if you have any concerns about other members of staff.

Propriety and behaviour

In your capacity as a professional working in a school, you should ensure that you act in a professional way at all times. When working with pupils we are required to behave in an appropriate way and with respect for others and make sure that children and young people also understand what is expected of them. As adults we are also role models and so should set an example through our own behaviour.

It is also important that pupils are aware of the boundaries of acceptable and unacceptable behaviour, both within and outside school as well as online. This means that they should know how to treat others and also know how they should expect to be treated.

You should be aware that, whilst pupils may come to you and seek advice and reassurance, you may need to consult with other staff as well as your school's child protection or safeguarding policy in order to ensure that you handle these correctly, especially if you suspect some kind of abuse (see Brilliant dos and don'ts below). If a pupil decides to confide in you about abuse, it is very important that you explain to them that you will need to tell another adult.

As well as listening to pupils who may confide in you, you should also be on the lookout for signs of abuse. Remember that there are different kinds of abuse which can also be passive, that is the abuser has neglected in their duty of care for the child, either physically or emotionally.

Brilliant dos and don'ts: Safeguarding

Do

- ✔ Tell pupils that they have done the right thing in talking to someone.
- ✔ Tell them that you believe them.
- ✔ Say that you will help them.

Don't

- ✗ Ask the pupil too many questions about what has happened.
- ✗ Make promises about what will or won't happen.
- ✗ Tell them that you won't tell anyone else.

After you have spoken with the pupil you will need to inform the designated member of staff for child protection or DSL – make sure you know who this person is in your school in case you need to speak to them urgently about a pupil. You should also make written notes of what the pupil has told you straightaway so that you can pass on the details as soon as possible.

The NSPCC has a large number of resources and advice on their website for children and young people as well as parents, carers and professionals.

Brilliant case study

Jack is working as a cover supervisor in key stage 3. He does not work with all the pupils as he tends to cover maths and music lessons, but this involves working with the same pupils each week. He has been approached by a pupil in Year 9 who has said that she is worried about her friend in her class whose father is an alcoholic – she says that her friend has confided in her that he is sometimes violent with both her and her mother.

- Outline what Jack should do.
- What should he say to each of the girls about the situation?

Providing pastoral support to pupils

Providing pastoral support may range from solving disagreements during breaktimes to concerns about homework, worries due to issues at home, or friendship and social problems. As well as providing general guidance, this may sometimes involve talking about quite complex issues which are happening in pupils' lives either within or outside school, such as bullying, bereavement, family breakdown, drug and alcohol dependency, or children as carers. In some cases, pupils' general behaviour will also be affected by these issues and you will need to be able to support them in managing their feelings. (See also Chapter 5.) Many young people now have social media accounts, which means that they are unable to escape from bullying, and online bullies may pick on individuals or groups in this way.

Adults in schools need to be approachable so that pupils can confide in them and feel that they will be supported. You may be approached in different situations and at different stages for advice, support and reassurance. Pupils may come to you simply because you are known to them, or because you work with them in this capacity, for example as a learning mentor or family worker, in which case you should have had some additional training – see examples below.

Brilliant examples

In Charlotte's primary school, she runs a 'Listening ear' club, which is open during morning break three times per week. The club is to encourage any pupils who need to talk to an adult to come and do this and to know that there is an adult there at set times who is able to listen. Charlotte has been able to talk to pupils who have worries and to support them in finding a way to work these through. She has been on additional training through the school and also holds a counselling qualification.

Charlie is a learning support assistant for Elysha in Year 7, who has sensory needs, and regularly works with whole groups of pupils, as well as the girl he supports. He is required to be on duty during breaktimes and lunchtimes and as a result frequently has to deal with disagreements and disputes by talking them through with pupils.

It is likely that you will also provide regular pastoral support to pupils during the school day – teaching assistants are often in a position to do this as they may have more time and opportunity than teachers. This is an integral part of your role and you will need to reassure pupils that it is good to talk about their feelings and that you will help them as much as you can.

Brilliant activity

Reflect on how many times during a normal day you are asked to intervene or support pupils in managing social issues or pupils' anxieties. Are you able to do this yourself or do you need to ask for the help of others?

Mentoring

Learning mentors were originally introduced into schools as part of the government's Excellence in Cities initiative in 2001. As part of the initiative, learning mentors were recruited to support schools in raising standards, improving attendance and reducing exclusions through working closely with individual pupils. The role of the learning mentor has become a key part of the role of some support staff, and some are employed with mentor as part of their job title. Learning mentors are involved in helping to remove barriers to learning and to raise pupil achievement in school with pupils of all ages. They will work alongside teachers to set targets and support pupils in developing their confidence and self-esteem, and looking at ways of improving their work. They will also work alongside parents and carers and may also run sessions to support them in school.

Brilliant example

Zak works in a large secondary school as a learning mentor. He works with groups of pupils and individuals, and also with teachers and the SENDCo to identify support strategies and build pupils' confidence and motivation.

The kinds of skills an effective mentor will need are an extension of those required for the role of teaching assistant. Learning mentors need to be good listeners, develop good relationships with their mentees and offer support through talking through issues. They will also need to be able to encourage and motivate pupils, in particular in cases of low self-esteem and disaffection with school. However, in order to be a learning mentor you should also be sent on specific training to ensure that you are fully prepared for your role.

The mentoring process should be regulated through your local authority and it is likely that there will be a link learning mentor who will be able to establish local networks and share good practice between schools and local services, as well as directing schools to other local and national groups. Learning mentors should not work in isolation and your school should set up an initial mentoring action plan after discussing the pupil's needs with their family and involving other services where these are needed (see Figure 4.3). Your role will include working with pupils on all aspects of school life, whether this is to do with learning, socialising with others, managing their own needs or with anger management issues.

Brilliant activity

Find some job descriptions for learning mentors online. What are their responsibilities?

Figure 4.3 Other services potentially involved

External services will work with the school to support and monitor the effectiveness of the mentoring process, in particular with regard to pupil progress and attendance. They may also provide resources and further training, as well as attending meetings between local mentoring cluster groups. If you are asked to be involved in mentoring, make sure that you find out as much as you can about both the pupil and the way in which the school manages the process. This may involve speaking to your school's SENDCo or inclusion manager about the kinds of activities you are to undertake with particular pupils and the time allocated to do this.

Working on PSHE activities with pupils

The subject of Personal, Social and Health Education (PSHE) often takes place alongside and through other subjects, or through the wider work of the school. PSHE is not a national curriculum subject, and schools are free to incorporate it into the curriculum to build on what is there. Through PSHE activities, pupils are encouraged to learn about themselves and how to keep safe, as well as developing skills and rules for keeping healthy such as physical activity and a healthy diet. They will be encouraged to develop social skills such as helping others, resolving their own arguments and resisting bullying, as well as making more informed choices about their own health and the environment. As they go through school, they will also learn about relationships and later sex education, which is compulsory for all pupils. As a teaching assistant, you will be unlikely to carry out PSHE activities on your own with pupils, although you will be present in the classroom when different aspects of it are taught.

Brilliant example

At Mine's primary school, a health bus comes to visit once a year and each class have a half hour slot during the day. They carry out age-related activities which reinforce what is being taught in school in a fun way using puppets and a short film. Mine goes with different classes in her year group (Year 2) and they have discussed different ways of keeping healthy, such as diet and exercise.

Brilliant activity

Find out how your school teaches PSHE and how many hours each week is dedicated to it.

Supporting transitions

Whatever age group you are working with, it is likely that at some stage you will be supporting them through different transitions or changes in their lives. Whether these changes are within the school environment or the outside world, you may need to prepare them for moving on or accepting a change in circumstances. Transitions can be quite traumatic for some pupils, and you will need to work closely with teachers to develop strategies to support pupils as they pass through transitions at different stages. In some of these situations, teachers may need to call on the help of mentors or other trained adults. There are different types of transitions – some of which are planned, and some of which are unplanned.

Examples of planned transitions might be:

- starting school
- moving classes
- adolescence
- leaving school

Examples of unplanned transitions might be:

- bereavement
- pregnancy
- changes to family structure
- illness
- moving house

Starting school

If you are working with the youngest age group in school, you will be involved in supporting pupils through one of the biggest changes they have experienced. The school will have a series of steps in place to ensure that children and families are supported through a time which can be a big change for both sides.

Usually when starting school, teachers will have visited either the child's home or Nursery if it is not attached to the school, so that they can be introduced to the child. They may also have a series of introductory sessions during the term before the child starts school so that children can experience being in school and meet some of their peers and existing Reception children, especially if they are starting school in January.

If you are working with this age group, make sure you spend plenty of time talking and getting to know pupils during the first few weeks of school, as well as carrying out the necessary observations and so gaining a clear picture of each child, particularly if you are their key worker. (For more on the EYFS, see Chapter 2.)

Moving classes

Reception to Year 1

The transition from Reception to Year 1 should not be as much of a challenge to pupils as their initial entry into school, in particular since the foundation stage curriculum is now extended for the first term that the child is in Year 1 as part of the transition process. However, although this is the case, Year 1 can still be very different. Pupils may not have participated in whole-school activities such as assemblies and breaktimes with older children, and there may be fewer adults in a Year 1 classroom. It is likely that at this time teachers in this year group will meet for a handover meeting to share information about each child and to discuss their foundation stage profiles, and to highlight children with special educational needs. This will then occur at the same time of year in subsequent changes of year group.

Brilliant tip

Whatever year group you support, ask if you can be present at this handover meeting at the start of the school year so that you can find out about the needs of the pupils in advance. If possible, also speak to your SENDCo about any pupils who have additional needs.

Year 2 to Year 3

Depending on the school or schools, the transfer from Year 2 to Year 3 may be no more of a challenge than any other year group. In many primary schools transferring to the juniors may simply be moving upstairs or to a different corridor. However, in some cases, pupils will be physically moving schools when transferring from key stage 1 to key stage 2. Even though these schools may be on the same site, they will frequently be housed in different buildings. In this situation or if pupils are changing sites, it is important for staff to manage the handover carefully and ensure that pupils have plenty of time both with their new teacher and have a chance to look around and speak to others in the school.

Year 6 to Year 7 (Primary to Secondary)

This transition is usually managed carefully as pupils will be starting a completely new phase in their schooling. If you are working in a Year 6 class it is likely that during the summer term you will be carrying out projects and activities and having discussions around the subject of secondary school. These activities will encourage pupils to start to focus on secondary school and also to talk about their concerns and any anxieties which they may have. Year 6 teachers will liaise with the head of year from Year 7 where possible to discuss the needs of pupils and to address any concerns. Similarly, the start of Year 7 will need to be managed carefully so that pupils learn to be more responsible for organising themselves around issues such as timetabling and homework, which will be difficult to start with.

Brilliant case study

Jean-Paul works in a small village primary school where the pupils usually transfer to a number of much larger secondary schools in the area. He spends his time as a teaching assistant in a mixed Year 5/6 class and is presently working with the teacher to manage the leavers' production and to ensure that the transition process goes smoothly.

- Why is it particularly important in Jean-Paul's school to manage transition actively and to reassure pupils about any concerns which they may have?
- How might Jean-Paul be involved in the process?

Adolescence

Before and during adolescence, children are having to manage the physical, social and emotional changes of the transition from a child to an adult. This can cause them to become anxious as well as affect their behaviour in school. Children and young people may find this easier by talking about what to expect, for example during Relationships and Sex Education (RSE) sessions.

Brilliant case study

Leanne is a teaching assistant in Years 5 and 6. The school nurse has come to speak to Year 6 about puberty and what they can expect to happen. The talk is happening separately for boys and girls. Some of the children have said to Leanne that they do not need to go to the talk as they already know what is going to happen as part of puberty.

- What should Leanne say to the children?
- Why is it important that they go to the talk?

Leaving school

This can be a difficult transition to manage as pupils will usually leave secondary school following their last exams. The process will need to be driven by teachers and support staff throughout the last year of school and in particular if pupils are intending to leave following GCSEs. You may be approached by pupils at this time if they are finding it difficult to decide which options to take and need some support in doing this. You may need to refer them to your school's careers teachers or for additional support outside school – in some areas of the country there is a Connexions service, which offers support and advice to 13- to 19-year-olds.

Unplanned transitions

Unplanned transitions can be more difficult to manage, as they are unexpected and are more likely to be traumatic as pupils will not have been prepared for them. In some cases, parents and carers may not have told schools what has happened and it is not until the pupil starts to talk about it or behaves differently that a problem is discovered. You should not be surprised if children and young people want to talk about these some time later as they may need to have time to process the information. In all cases, staff will need to work with families to provide support during:

- bereavement
- pregnancy

- changes to family structure
- illness
- moving house

Bereavement

Bereavement may take many forms, and if the pupil has lost a close family member or friend it is likely to impact significantly on the child or young person. Depending on how close the person was, the pupil may also need to have some time out of school, which will have a knock on effect on their academic progress. As a teaching assistant your role will be to give pupils the opportunity to talk about their feelings and ask questions.

Pregnancy

If you are working in a secondary school, you may be approached by pupils who have become pregnant. In this situation, they will need to have opportunities to talk about the choices available to them and support in making decisions, as well as having discussions with parents and carers and seeking advice from outside agencies such as the NHS.

Changes to family structure

Changes may be caused by the departure of a parent or the introduction of a step parent, possibly with their own child, a new baby or grandparents. These kinds of changes may not outwardly affect the child, but in some cases their reaction may be quite severe, particularly if it relates to their parents or carers.

Brilliant case study

Joseph is in your class in Reception and has always been happy and settled. However, for the past week his behaviour has been very different. He has been unable to concentrate on anything and has been repeatedly pushing other children and taking things away from them. The teacher has asked his mum to come in after school to talk about his behaviour and she tells her that Joseph's father moved out last week and that her boyfriend has moved into their home.

- Why is it important for the teacher to talk this through with Joseph's mum?
- How can you and the teacher support Joseph?

Illness

Sometimes children or young people and their parents or carers may suffer from illness which is long term or which causes them to miss significant time off school. In some cases, they may be young carers who need to look after parents or carers who are ill. You may need to help teachers to prepare work which they can do at home and send it to them, or arrange a buddy system to keep them in touch with what is happening in school.

Moving house

Sometimes moving house has been planned for a long time but in other cases, children may be moved from temporary accommodation, which means that it happens more quickly. They may also have the stress of not knowing how long they will be in their accommodation/location or be fleeing from conflict situations which are traumatic. In this situation, all staff should be aware so that the pupil is given the support they need as well as an acknowledgement that they may find it difficult to think about school work.

Brilliant recap

- Make sure you always take the time to listen to pupils and get to know them.
- Follow up on any issues which pupils have discussed with you.

- Be alert to any safeguarding or child protection issues and report concerns to your DSL immediately.
- Keep up to date with safeguarding legislation and guidance and attend all training.
- Work with teachers to ensure transitions are managed effectively as far as possible.
- Seek training if you are involved in additional strategies for supporting pastoral care such as mentoring.

Further reading

Keeping Children Safe in Education (DfE, 2023): Statutory guidance for practitioners.

What to do if you are worried a child is being abused: Advice for Practitioners (HM Government 2015).

Working Together to Safeguard Children (HM Government 2023).

www.gov.uk/government/publications/prevent-duty-guidance-for-england-and-wales

www.kidscape.org.uk – A charity to prevent bullying and child abuse

www.childnet.com/teachers-and-professionals/ – this website provides help for specific safeguarding queries.

www.ceop.gov.uk – (Child Exploitation and Online Protection Centre) – Organisation which aims to provide information to parents and carers, children and education professionals around safety online. It also allows anyone to report online abuse.

www.nspcc.org.uk – the NSPCC website contains a wide range up-to-date information on safeguarding for parents, children and professionals.

www.childline.org.uk – information and advice for children and young people.

PSHE Association – www.pshe-association.org.uk

Brook advisory service (pregnancy support) – www.brook.org.uk

Family lives – support for young parents – www.familylives.org.uk

Chapter 5

Supporting pupil behaviour and self-regulation

All adults who work in schools will need to know about and understand strategies to manage pupils' behaviour and support them in managing their feelings and emotions. The whole school team will need to be able to implement agreed school strategies as part of a consistent approach to encourage positive behaviour whilst supporting pupil emotional responses.

Research from a survey on the Mental Health of Children and Young People living in England (MHCYP) in 2022 has shown that since the Covid-19 pandemic, 18% of children and young people between the ages of 7 and 16 years have a probable mental disorder (Digital NHS UK, 2023: https://digital.nhs.uk/). This is an increase from 12.1% when using the same survey in 2017. The report also states that 61.2% of 11- to 16-year-olds are less likely to feel safe in school. These results mean that in classrooms, more pupils will be facing challenges and this will mean that they are likely to find it harder to concentrate.

We call the ability to control our impulse and emotions self-regulation, and children and young people are less likely to be able to do this when they are feeling stressed, challenged or anxious. We should always remember that behaviour is a form of communication and the reason for it is unlikely to be apparent, as it will be communicating an emotional need.

Brilliant example

A pupil who is displaying inappropriate behaviour in a school setting may not be doing this as a matter of choice. They are responding to the way they are feeling.

You may be asked to support pupil behaviour in a variety of contexts, including around the school, during lunchtimes, on school trips and in different learning environments. As a member of staff, you should be able to show that you are aware of your school's behaviour or self-regulation policy and are part of this approach to managing behaviour. You should also be able to talk pupils through reasons for negative behaviour so that they can start to understand why they are feeling the way they do (sometimes known as co-regulation). This will help them to develop self-awareness and start to learn how to reflect and self-regulate. Some schools are therefore moving away from a traditional 'behaviour management' approach of sanctions and strategies for pupils as it is felt that they do not address their anxieties or help them to feel calm. In this case, they may take the approach of the four 'zones of regulation', which were devised by Leah Kuypers in her book of the same name.

The zones of regulation

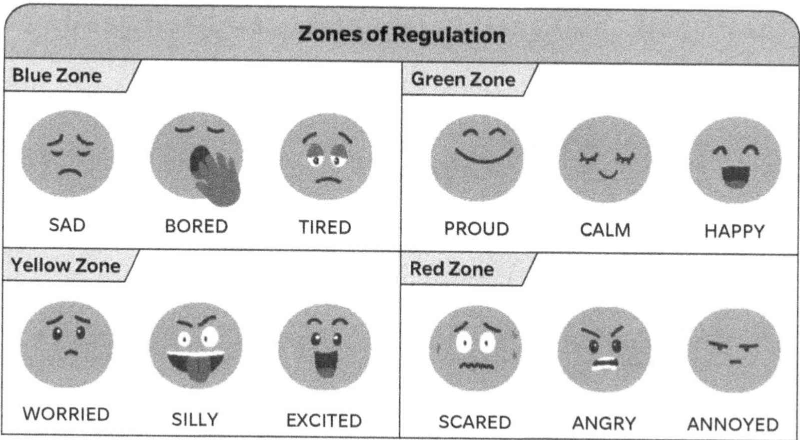

Figure 5.1 Zones of regulation

The four zones of regulation (see Figure 5.1) provide a useful tool when supporting pupils in being able to use the skill of self-regulation. Although they should be used differently with pupils of different ages and stages of emotional development, they give us a starting point for modelling the types of skills and language that we need to use when managing emotions such as anger, frustration, sadness and so on.

The role of the adult is important – by talking to pupils about the reasons for their feelings, we will help them to start to understand why they are feeling the way they do and be able to talk about it. Ultimately, we need pupils to take responsibility for their own behaviour within the framework of the school code of conduct and through being part of the wider school community.

Brilliant tip

The next time you need to address a behaviour issue, focus on the reason for it rather than the behaviour, for example, start by saying, 'What has upset you? Are you are upset because they wouldn't let you play with them?

Brilliant activity

Research more about self-regulation and co-regulation and the reasons for giving children and young people opportunities to self-reflect and take ownership of their feelings.

The importance of an agreed code of conduct

Whether the school uses a policy of sanctions and strategies or methods of self-regulation, pupils will need to understand the school's expectations for behaviour and the reasons that these expectations exist. All schools will have an agreed code of conduct which pupils know and refer to regularly; this is important so that pupils know what is expected of them.

In schools where self-regulation is being used as a strategy, there may be a list of strategies which are used when pupils need additional support with their behaviour, such as time out with an adult, learning mentor or buddy.

Although all schools will have 'school rules' (Figure 5.2) it is also likely that individual classes or subjects will also have their own agreed codes of conduct – for example, in a chemistry lab or an outdoor area. It is helpful if pupils can be involved in devising these rules to draw attention to them and also so that they have more ownership of them.

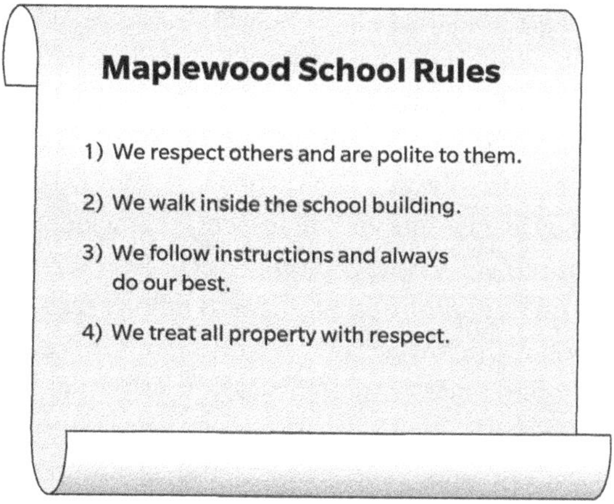

Maplewood School Rules

1) We respect others and are polite to them.
2) We walk inside the school building.
3) We follow instructions and always do our best.
4) We treat all property with respect.

Figure 5.2 Maplewood school rules

Brilliant case study

Year 5 have been in the class for almost half a term and the class teacher and teaching assistant have devised an agreed set of rules with the children, which are displayed on the wall. There have been a number of issues within the class between the children and one particular child, Ralf, seems to be at the centre of most of the incidents. The class teacher says to him, 'Ralf, we agreed as a class that we will always be kind to others.'

- Do you think that Ralf will be more likely to listen to the teacher since he helped devise the rules?
- What else could staff do to try to ensure that this kind of behaviour occurs less frequently?

Factors impacting on pupil behaviour

As you will know, reasons for pupils' inappropriate or negative behaviour relate to their feelings and may be complex (see Figure 5.3). Remember also that the kind of behaviour to look out for in school may not just be the loud or attention-seeking kind – behaviour can also be withdrawn or passive. Pupils' home and social experiences will have a huge impact on the way in which they relate and react to others, and while most pupils will want to gain positive adult attention, those who behave inappropriately are usually trying to do this in a negative way. They will also be affected by arguments with their peers, or incidents at home.

It is important to get to know pupils and to find out about their backgrounds and personalities as this will help you to look out for behaviour which is uncharacteristic; finding out more about them may also help you to understand why they may behave in a particular way. Although you may not have any control over some of these contributing factors, knowing about them will help you to support pupils in self-regulating and understanding why they feel the way they do.

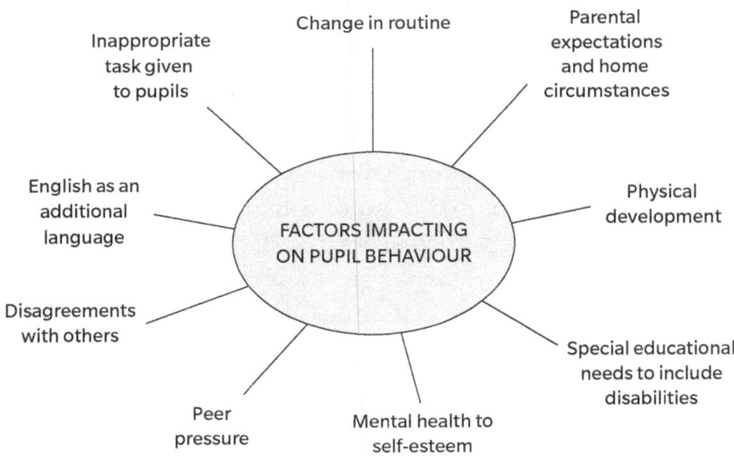

Figure 5.3 Factors impacting on pupil behaviour

Parental expectations and home circumstances

Parents and carers will vary a great deal in their expectations of what is right for their child. Depending on the level of discipline which they have had growing up, the extremes may be that they are very strict or make too many allowances for their child's behaviour. Some parents or carers may also lack confidence and ask for advice from school staff about how to manage their child's behaviour at home. These parental factors will clearly make a difference to how a pupil behaves. You may also find that pupils say to you '. . . but I am allowed to do that/say that at home' when you speak to them about their behaviour. Remember that parental expectations are likely to vary considerably – what is acceptable at home may not be acceptable in the school environment or in wider society. The answer to this is that we do not behave in this way in school.

Psychologists talk about different parenting styles which have an impact on the way in which they manage behaviour. This may affect children and young people's responses to adult intervention at school.

Permissive

This type of parent or carer does not apply boundaries or enforce strategies to manage behaviour. They are likely to avoid confrontation with their child which may mean that the child is not used to rules as they are used to 'getting their own way.'

Brilliant example

Lexi is 4 and is just starting school. She has an older brother and lives with her parents who both bring her to school in the mornings. You have noticed that she is not used to doing anything for herself. She is unable to put on her cardigan, coat or shoes without help and changing for PE is a challenge for her. Lexi can also be quite defiant towards adults, often refusing to carry out instructions and work with the rest of the class. One adult has to stay with her throughout changing times, which means that they are unable to help anyone else.

Authoritative

This type of parent or carer sets clear rules for their child and shares expectations for behaviour with them. They are good communicators who listen to their child, provide guidance and encourage discussion. They consider their child's thoughts and feelings and are honest and open with them.

Neglectful

This type of parent or carer is absent or not involved with their child's social/emotional or behavioural needs and does not provide guidance or understanding when managing their behaviour. They may have self-esteem issues themselves or be struggling with their own mental health.

Authoritarian

This type of parent or carer will apply strict rules and punishments for their child if they break them. There is unlikely to be any communication with the child about why rules are needed and enforced. There is little justification for their demands as the parent wants to be in control.

Brilliant case study

Josh is in Year 7 and is struggling to manage his behaviour. This takes the form of regular fights during breaktimes, and frustration and loud name calling within the classroom. The SENDCo has asked his parents to come in for a meeting with his form teacher and year group leader and it is clear that his father, who does most of the parenting due to his mother's long work hours, is very strict with Josh at home.

- What type of parenting style is being demonstrated here?
- Do you think that it is the cause of Josh's poor behaviour in school?
- How might the school and Josh's parents work together to support him?

Although parenting styles may have features of more than one of these types, they will still affect the way in which children respond to expectations of behaviour in school. Of the four styles, it is generally accepted that those who lean towards the more authoritative style will raise independent children who are able to self-regulate.

When thinking about pupils' behaviour, you should also remember that sadly a significant number of children are victims of some form of abuse – this may be verbal, physical, sexual or through neglect – and this is highly likely to affect their behaviour. The NSPCC reported that in 2021–22, half a million children a year suffered from abuse in the UK (see Chapter 4 on Safeguarding for more about forms of abuse). Look out for quiet and withdrawn behaviour, or pupils who seem preoccupied, and of course if you have concerns, always speak to your school's DSL.

Self-esteem and mental health issues

Our self-esteem can be high or low, positive or negative. It is how we feel about ourselves that leads to our self-image – that is, how we think about or perceive ourselves. Children develop positive self-esteem when they feel good about themselves and when they feel valued. As there are more children and young people than ever before in schools who are struggling with anxiety and mental health issues, as educators it is important that we recognise that pupils' outward behaviour is often a reaction to how they are feeling. In addition, helping them to talk through how they are feeling as part of co-regulation strategies will empower them and help improve their emotional vocabulary. We must also value each child as an individual and celebrate differences and similarities.

Brilliant tip

Always make time to check in with quieter pupils, ask them how they are, and remember things which are important to them. In this way you will develop a relationship with them which will help and reassure them.

Peer pressure

Pupils may be influenced negatively or positively by their peers. In a negative way, pressure may be put on them to conform to certain behaviour to be part of a group, particularly as they go through secondary school. This can in turn cause a conflict within the pupil if the behaviour goes against their own conscience. Wanting to be part of the group may also influence them in a positive way, for example if they want to be seen as doing the right thing by their friends.

Brilliant case study

Marwa is in Year 9 and has recently come to your school following a house move. She has been in school for two months and there are serious concerns about her behaviour which is defiant towards adults, as she often refuses to carry out instructions or work with others. She has not responded to any of the school's strategies for managing behaviour, has not made many friends and is quite isolated during breaks. Teachers have met her mother and the SENDCo but have been told that Marwa's behaviour is fine at home although she is concerned. The school has not had Marwa's records from her previous school.

- Why might Marwa be displaying this type of behaviour in school?
- How might you and the teacher support Marwa?

Disagreements with others

If pupils have had an argument or are upset about something which has happened at breaktime for example, they may well be affected by it during lesson time. You may find that pupils come in from break and are very quiet, or are upset in some way – never ignore this even if it means delaying what you are going to do – you should always speak to the pupils and discuss what has happened.

Brilliant example

Sanjit is working in a Year 5 class as a teaching assistant. One of the children, Alfie, is working as part of a group on a collaborative activity and the children need to listen to one another's ideas and work together. Alfie has become upset and is not engaging with the others at all; he eventually storms off and says that he doesn't want to do it as nobody is listening to him. According to the school behaviour policy, Alfie should be given a verbal warning and have his name put on the board.

- Can you think of another course of action for Alfie?
- How might this help him in the future?

Special educational needs and disabilities

Depending on their social and emotional needs, pupils may find some aspects of learning and expectations of behaviour difficult, which may have an impact on their behaviour. In some cases they may also have a behaviour plan and in this case you will need to know what is in it if you are working with them (see also Chapter 6).

English as an additional language (EAL)

Ensure that any pupils you are supporting have an understanding of acceptable behaviour, and that you are clear with them why there is a problem with their behaviour in case there are gaps in their understanding. Sometimes frustration about being unable to communicate clearly with others can also cause them to behave inappropriately (see Chapter 7 for more on working with pupils with EAL).

Inappropriate task given to pupils

If the task which pupils have been given to do is too easy or difficult for them, they may not be engaged in what they are doing. This may make them start to look for other things to do or distract others. Teachers should have given the pupils extension tasks if they are able to complete quickly, and they may need to be reminded of this. If the task is too difficult, it may need to be broken down into smaller steps so that pupils are able to understand what to do next.

A change in routine

Sometimes a transition such as a change in routine may be all that is needed to provoke changes to pupil behaviour. They may be excitable due to a school trip or another situation which is a change from the norm. You can anticipate this as you become more experienced and be ready for it!

Physical development

If pupils are very different physically from their peers due to, for example, different growth patterns, their behaviour may be affected. They may also be treated differently by their peers due to their height or weight. You may need to make additional provision when Year 6 are getting changed for PE, for example, as puberty is likely to have started in many cases.

Working in groups

Pupils will sometimes need to work with adults in groups, sometimes for a series of lessons or on intervention work. If you are the supporting adult in this situation you should always speak to pupils before starting the first session about what kinds of group rules you should have, and record them so that they are available for future sessions. In this way you are making the pupils aware of your expectations as well as those of their peers. If you find that you have a particular pupil or pupils who are disrupting the rest of the group you may need to give them time out so that you can talk to them later about what has happened and why they have caused a disruption.

Brilliant activity

Think about what you do when you are feeling upset or angry. How do you control your feelings? What do you do to help you feel better?

School policy for behaviour and self-regulation

Your school's behaviour or self-regulation policy should set out the strategies which are available to you to use as a member of staff. It is important that all adults have read and/or had training on the expectations and responsibilities of staff when doing this. This training may need to be updated regularly so that all new staff are also clear on the school's approach. If you have any worries or concerns about how to deal with specific behaviour you should always refer to a teacher or your school SENDCo.

Depending upon the age and/or needs of pupils, the strategies available to you may be very different – this is to ensure that they are age appropriate and incorporate the school's approach towards pupil behaviour. Your school should have strategies which are clear and which take the pupils' age and needs into account. There should also be clear guidance in the case of bullying, racist, physical violence or abusive behaviour.

You should also check to see whether rewards are given to pupils for effort and behaviour – this might take the form of merit marks, team points, stickers, certificates and so on. It is unlikely that as a teaching assistant you will be unable to apply particular strategies or rewards but you should check – in case, for example, only teachers can use them.

Brilliant activity

Using a copy of your school's behaviour or self-regulation policy, highlight or note down:

- your responsibilities under the policy
- rewards which are used in the school (team points, stickers, etc.)
- strategies which you can use (brain breaks, using sensory calming kits, etc.)
- how positive behaviour is promoted

Positive behaviour management

Positive behaviour management is a focus on the positive aspects of what a pupil is doing. An example of this might be if, when speaking to pupils, we ignore inappropriate behaviour and focus on those pupils who are doing the right thing: 'Well done, Ryan, for sitting beautifully' may make others do the same in order to gain your attention.

There are a number of different ways in which adults can promote positive behaviour in schools. This is important, particularly when staff are working with specific pupils who have dysregulated behaviour (see below). We will all dwell on and think about negative comments which are made about us and children are no different; however, research has shown that we need to be given six positive comments for every negative one in order to redress the balance. It can be much easier for us to focus on the negative aspects of a pupil's behaviour and react to it because we are annoyed, although this can often make the situation worse. We should think about why we are reacting to them in the way that we are and consider how we can support them rather than do this. Praise and positive behaviour strategies will be beneficial to pupils and schools for a number of reasons:

- they create a positive environment for staff and pupils
- they provide motivation for pupils through positive encouragement and rewards
- they make pupils feel noticed
- they increase pupils' self-esteem and confidence

How can we promote positive behaviour?

Model expected behaviour

As adults we should always model the kind of behaviour we expect from pupils. Good role models will set an example to pupils and show them how to behave and relate to others. An example of this might be when we are in assembly and chatting to other staff before it starts. If pupils see us doing this they are far less likely to do it themselves – the rule is no talking, so why are adults doing it?

Notice when pupils are trying hard and use positive language

Effort is just as important as achievement – it is important to keep an eye out for occasions when a pupil is really working on their behaviour or trying hard academically, particularly if they find either of these things difficult. Always be clear on any behaviour you are describing and focus on this rather than the pupil, for example 'I noticed that you tried really hard to do the right thing just now'. Recognising that pupils are managing their feelings when they have found it difficult in the past will also support them and show them that you are noticing their efforts.

Show pupils respect

As adults we need to have good manners and show respect to others, being mindful of the importance of being inclusive. This is very important – we need to show the same respect that we are asking pupils to show so that we can support them and build positive relationships with everyone.

You should also be very aware of your own assumptions and prejudices and avoid using them in a school context. Stereotyping pupils can limit their development just as they are starting to build their own ideas. If they hear adults making prejudicial remarks they will grow up thinking that there is no harm in that type of behaviour. The pupils who are the subject of the remarks will also be damaged further by the reinforcement of low expectations and low self-esteem. Beware of stereotyping pupils even through comments such as 'I need some sensible girls to take this message for me' – this may sound to boys as though only girls can be sensible. Also, never assume that pupils with special educational needs do not understand situations or are unable to complete tasks – include everyone as much as you can. (See also Chapter 7 for more on equity and diversity in schools.)

Use positive recognition

As well as using verbal praise, as a teaching assistant you should also be able to use merit marks and other rewards which celebrate good work and behaviour, for example through celebration assemblies and open days. Make sure, particularly with younger pupils or those who have special educational needs, that you tell them exactly why you are praising them as they may not always understand why. You can say 'I am giving you this award because you have worked so hard on your maths this term.'

Give responsibilities to pupils

This is very effective since it reinforces the pupil's self-esteem and also encourages them to think about the positive effects of helping others. For example, many schools now have school councils which give some responsibility to pupils and gives them opportunities to think about and discuss whole school issues, and make decisions within the boundaries of the school environment.

> **Brilliant activity**
>
> Consider what you do in your school to encourage positive behaviour and encourage pupils to make good choices.

Follow up on issues which are important

You should always follow up on issues, particularly if you have made a point of saying you will. If you see Becky behaving very well in the corridor and say that you will tell her teacher how pleased you are, you must remember to do it. If you do not, there is an implication that you do not see it as important and she may be less likely to behave well again.

Building a positive environment

Your school may also have additional frameworks in place to support a positive environment. It is important that we give pupils the opportunity to talk about their feelings and how these affect their behaviour. In addition, an important part of the learning process encourages pupils to make choices for themselves, as shown through assessment for learning and looking at how they are moving towards personalised targets and goals. A positive environment also means somewhere that pupils can put forward their ideas for discussion without fear of being criticised or having their feelings ignored.

Brilliant tip

When working with experienced teachers, take note of how they manage behaviour in different situations and try out some of their strategies yourself where appropriate.

Brilliant dos and don'ts

Do

- ✔ Have high but realistic expectations of work and behaviour.
- ✔ Create a positive learning environment and value pupils' work and achievements.
- ✔ Be clear and consistent with school expectations.
- ✔ Remember to notice and praise positive behaviour and self-regulation.

Don't

- ✗ Make assumptions about people – be aware of your own values and opinions.
- ✗ 'Pick' on pupils or look for them misbehaving. Catch them being good instead!
- ✗ Be surprised if a strategy which worked before doesn't work today – when managing behaviour you will need to have different approaches.

Working with individual pupils who have dysregulated behaviour

You may, as a teaching assistant, have been employed specifically to work with a pupil who consistently has dysregulated behaviour. As discussed earlier in the chapter, this may be caused by a number of factors or conditions. In this situation you should have clear guidance and support from your school's SENDCo and from others who work with the pupil. It is likely that they have an EHCP or Behaviour Support Plan and there will be advice available from other agencies who have worked with the pupil. These may be:

- **Educational psychologists (EPs):** These professionals visit schools regularly to work with and support pupils and the adults who work with them. They offer help and advice on a variety of issues and may also carry out assessments and programmes to support pupils who have special educational needs.
- **Local behaviour support teachers:** Behaviour support teachers will be based at the local education authority and can be brought in by the school to give advice and support for pupils who may have problems regulating their behaviour. They may be able to come in and work individually with pupils or to observe and offer suggestions to staff (see also Chapter 6 on supporting pupils who have special educational needs).

Brilliant tips

- Intervene as soon as you can to prevent the situation from becoming worse.
- You may not need to say anything – sometimes eye contact and the right expression can prevent unwanted behaviour.

- Ignore some behaviour if possible; sometimes distraction works with younger pupils.
- Remove any items which a pupil may be using inappropriately or as a distraction.
- Relate any comments to the behaviour rather than the pupil ('David, that was not a sensible idea') and avoid telling the pupil they are not sensible.
- Be realistic about pupil behaviour – do not sit pupils together if they usually find it hard to work productively together!

When working with pupils who have issues around behaviour, you should try to develop positive relationships with them. As a member of support staff you are well placed to spend time talking to the pupil and to find out about their needs and interests. You can also find out about the pupil through speaking to your SENDCo or talking to the pupil's parents or carers, or through discussions with teachers.

Remember, however, that you will need to be mindful of confidentiality and should not take any school records or reports off site. You should also not pass on any information about pupils to those who do not have a valid reason to know it.

When working with pupils who have behavioural needs you may also be involved in drawing up or using Education and Health Care Plans (EHCPs), Behaviour Support Plans (BSPs), Individual Education Plans (IEPs) or Personal Support Plans (PSPs), which will give targets for their behaviour. These documents will all follow similar formats but will include two or three targets to be worked on over the following weeks. You will then need to agree a further date to meet and review the pupil's progress. Depending on the pupil's needs, the SENDCo and parents or carers may also be present. The pupil should also always be there – even from an early age – so that they can be part of the process.

Managing challenging behaviour

At some stage all school staff will come up against behaviour which is challenging and which may in some cases be aggressive or a risk to the pupil or others. In this situation you will need to keep your wits about you and be very clear on your school's policy. Pupils may not always be aware of risks and dangerous situations, so when speaking to them you may need to point out the consequences of what they are doing. You should also be aware of your own responsibilities – if things have already got out of hand or if you are at all concerned you should send for another member of staff straightaway. You should also always seek help if:

- you or others are in any danger
- pupils are behaving unpredictably or aggressively
- pupils are not carrying out your instructions and you are not in control of the situation

Your school's behaviour or self-regulation policy should also give guidelines for managing dysregulated behaviour. You may also need to use restraint to prevent pupils from causing injury to themselves or others, but you should be careful when doing this and again have read your school's or local guidelines – restraint should be used as a last resort.

Brilliant case study

Sheila is working in the EYFS in her school and moves between the Nursery and Reception classes. In one of her groups is a child who regularly runs out of class, lashes out and often strikes other children and adults. The child is not able to focus on tasks or sit with other children. The class teacher has called a meeting with the child's foster parents, the SENDCo and all those who work with her.

- What might be the first steps in this situation?
- What else can the school do to support this pupil?

Working with pupils on restorative justice

One of the most challenging aspects of school for some pupils is to learn how to understand and respect the feelings of others. Young children in particular may find this difficult as their maturity and understanding are not developed enough for them to put themselves in the position of others. We often speak to them in school about how they should consider the consequences of their actions and how these may have affected others, but this can be difficult if they do not understand and recognise the reasons for their own feelings. Through stories, assemblies and role play and during circle time and PSHE and Citizenship activities we might encourage them to think about others' feelings.

Restorative justice is a strategy which has been applied in schools following its successful implementation in the criminal justice system, both at home and abroad. It has worked well as a method of resolving behaviour issues and learning from the consequences. Restorative justice is a helpful method of demonstrating to pupils what impact their behaviour will have on others through encouraging both parties to sit together and talk about what has happened. This method of conflict resolution has become a tried and tested means of supporting pupils through issues such as bullying and restoring positive relationships. It may take place through PSHE and SEAL sessions, assemblies and role play, or through focused group sessions which develop pupils' ability to listen to others and respect their feelings. Restorative justice sessions can be run by any trained member of school staff and will be slightly different in primary and secondary schools, although they follow the same principles. They may be run with small or large groups, so may be just two people with a mediator, or a circle time session to deal with problem solving.

Brilliant case study

Amal has been working in a secondary school for four months and is based in Years 7 and 8. He has been trained in restorative justice techniques at his previous school and also speaks Hindi. There have been some cases of racist bullying amongst the girls in the two year groups during breaktimes and Amal suggests to the head of Year 7 that he should run some sessions.

- What should Amal do first?
- What kind of form could the sessions take?

Brilliant activity

Look at the examples here and think about which you would be able to manage on your own and which you think you would need to refer to others:

- A playground argument between two Year 6 boys which has become aggressive.
- One of the pupils in your group is extremely quiet today and when you question her at the end of the session she starts crying and says she is being bullied.
- A pupil in Reception is having a full-blown temper tantrum because her childminder has just left and has taken her favourite blanket with her.
- A Year 8 pupil has become very angry during a group session with you and has stormed out.
- A special needs child has refused to take part in an activity with you because he doesn't want to.

How would you deal with those situations you could manage on your own?

Brilliant recap

- Make sure you have read and follow your school's behaviour/self-regulation policy.
- Be clear on what to do when you need to work with a pupil to manage their behaviour.
- Always set up ground rules when you start working with a new group.
- Make sure you have as much information and advice as possible when working with a pupil who finds it difficult to regulate their behaviour.
- Always refer to others in situations which are potentially dangerous.

Further reading

Conkbayir, Mine (2023) *The Neuroscience of the Developing Child*, Routledge.

Kuypers, Leah (2011) *The Zones of Regulation*, Think Social Publishing.

Chapter 6

Working with pupils who have Special Educational Needs and Disabilities

If you are working as a teaching assistant, it is likely that as part of your role you will at some stage be asked to support pupils who have special educational needs and disabilities, also known as SEND. You may do this because you are employed specifically to support an individual pupil as a learning support assistant or individual support assistant; however, you may also need to work with individuals or groups who need additional adult help in order to have full access to the curriculum. In order to do this, you will need to have skills in a number of areas, both in your relationships with others such as teachers, parents or carers and other professionals, as well as having empathy and understanding for the pupils you support. It may be that you develop a high level of responsibility, particularly if you are working with an individual pupil, as you will get to know them and their specific needs and develop partnerships with others who support them.

SEND Code of Practice 0–25 years

The term 'Special Educational Need' is defined by the SEND Code of Practice 2014 as 'a learning difficulty or disability which calls for special educational provision to be made for him or her'. The Code of Practice is a document which sets out clearly how the provision for pupils with special educational needs and disabilities should be managed within schools, academies, colleges and local authorities, as well as early years settings which are funded by local authorities.

The SEND Code of Practice is based on the legislation in Section 19 of the Children and Families Act 2014. If you are working with a pupil who has SEND, you should be familiar with the principles of the Code as local authorities must have regard to the following:

- The views, wishes and feelings of the child or young person, and the child's parents.
- The importance of the child or young person, and the child's parents, participating as fully as possible in decisions, and being provided with the information and support necessary to enable participation in those decisions.
- The need to support the child or young person, and the child's parents, in order to facilitate the development of the child or young person and to help them achieve the best possible educational and other outcomes, preparing them effectively for adulthood.

These principles focus on the child or young person and identify the steps which should be taken by schools and local authorities in order to support them and their families effectively. Schools should work with pupils and parents or carers in order to ensure that as far as possible the needs of children and young people are met in mainstream schools. Your role according to the code of practice is to work closely with the pupil and with parents or carers, teaching staff and other professionals in order to do this.

Brilliant tip

If you are working in a school and are supporting pupils with SEND, you do not need to read the whole SEND Code of Practice. However, it may be helpful to look at the chapters dealing with schools (Chapter 4) and how EHCPs are written (Chapter 9).

The SEND Code of Practice provides clear information and support so that parents, carers and all those who work with children and young people up to the age of 25 are able to work together to improve outcomes for those with SEND. It emphasises the importance of early identification and calls for a graduated response in the identification and support of pupils with additional needs in schools, colleges and early years settings. This means that there will be four stages of action whenever a concern is raised: this takes the form of assess, plan, do and review.

Assess

Firstly, if the school, college or early years setting have any concerns and feel that a pupil needs SEN support, the teacher should speak to their Special Educational Needs and Disabilities Co-Ordinator (SENDCo) and the child's parents or carers to carry out an assessment of the needs of the child. This will include as much information as possible from the parents or carers, the school and from previous assessments which have taken place. In the case of secondary schools, assessments from all subjects should be taken into account. The views of the child will also need to be considered. This should then provide information so that the setting can put interventions in place and should be reviewed regularly. If there is little or no improvement over time, a further assessment from external specialists may be needed such as health, social services or others with parental agreement.

Brilliant case study

Sue is working in a secondary school as a teaching assistant and cover supervisor. She has concerns about one of the boys in Year 8 due to his behaviour, but as Sue is based in different departments and works with different teachers, she is not sure who to discuss her concerns with.

- What should Sue do first?
- Why is it important that she says something?

Plan

The school, SENDCo, and parents or carers should meet to agree what outcomes they would like for the child and the provision or further interventions which are to be put in place. Again, this should also include the views of the child where possible. If staff need training or further support, this should also be provided.

Do

The class or subject teacher, along with the SENDCo, will monitor the pupil's progress and may be supported closely by teaching assistants or other specialist staff to ensure that interventions are linked to classroom teaching.

Review

The pupil's progress should be reviewed so that parents or carers and professionals can evaluate the support and its impact. The views of the pupil should again be considered at the review, and their needs should be analysed and revised, so that any changes can be made to the support provided. In cases where the pupil has an EHCP, this must be reviewed as a minimum every twelve months.

Education health care needs assessment

If the pupil is still not making progress despite the steps which have been put in place, the school and parents or carers may decide to apply for an education health care (EHC) assessment through the local authority. When applying for an EHC needs assessment, schools, parents or carers, or young people between 16 and 25 will need to present a case to their local authority to show that they need to have special educational provision made for them. The information which is gathered should outline the measures which have already been taken to support the child or young person. The local authority will take into account the wishes of the child or young person as well as their parents or carers, and decide whether they need to have special educational provision in the form of an Education Health Care Plan (EHCP). They will need to make a decision on whether this is needed within six weeks.

Not all EHC assessments will mean that the pupil is given an EHCP, and the local authority may decide that it is not appropriate. However, if the evidence provided indicates that one is needed, the pupil, parents or carers and school should be notified and a draft EHCP should be provided within twenty weeks of the initial request for assessment. All those who are working with the pupil should be invited to contribute to this.

Brilliant activity

Using Chapter 9 of the SEND Code of Practice 2014, find out what is involved in writing an EHCP and how the content is agreed.

The Local Offer

Another aspect of the Code of Practice is that all local authorities are required to publish a Local Offer, which sets out in one place the provision that is in place locally across education, health and social care for children and young people who have special educational needs and disabilities. The Local Offer should be published online and should also be accessible to those who do not have access to the internet.

Brilliant activity

Find a copy of the Local Offer in your area. What is available for children and young people who have special educational needs and disabilities? What can you specifically find out about educational provision?

Brilliant case study

Andre is working in Year 1 as a general teaching assistant. A child in the class, Phoebe, showed some causes for concern due to her speech and language, which is also impacting significantly on her ability to learn. After some discussion with the SENDCo and Phoebe's parents they decided initially to work on some specific language targets supported by her parents at home. Andre has been working with Phoebe three times a week for two terms on her targets, but Phoebe has made little progress when they come to Phoebe's review. At the review Phoebe's parents, the SENDCo and class teacher decide that they will refer Phoebe to a speech and language therapist for further assessment.

- If Phoebe does not progress further following speech and language therapy, what would be the next steps?

> **Brilliant activity**
>
> Find a copy of the SEND Code of Practice 2014. Look at Chapter 9 – what does it say about requesting an Education, Health and Care Needs assessment?

Knowing about the needs of the pupil you support

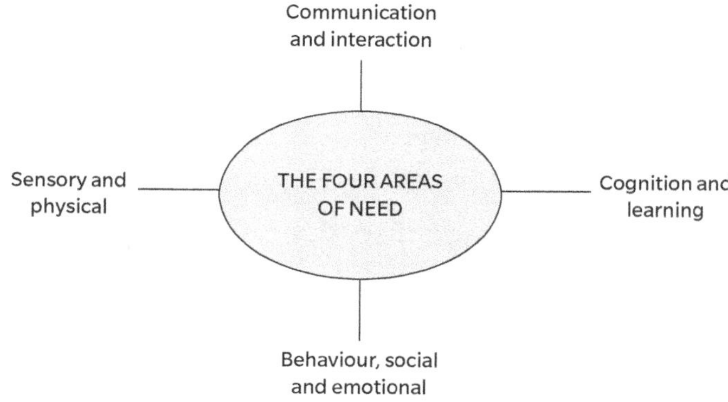

Figure 6.1 The four broad areas of special educational need

If you are supporting a pupil who has special educational needs, you will need to know about and be able to respond to their specific needs. The Code of Practice sets out four broad areas of special educational need (see Figure 6.1), and although each pupil will be different and their needs often relate to more than one area, it is helpful to have some idea of how their requirements are outlined. In each case the needs of the pupil may be moderate, severe or profound; in other words, they may only be slight or they may impact on the child or young person in all that they do. The four areas of need are as follows:

Communication and interaction

This means that the pupil has speech, language and communication needs (sometimes called SLCN). If a child has difficulties with speech and language, their hearing will be checked first to rule out any hearing issues.

Children with speech, language and communication needs may have problems in getting across their intended meaning, in understanding what others are saying to them or have difficulties with the social aspects of communication. This may be due to a speech and language delay, impairment or disorder, which will affect their ability to communicate with others. Pupils will need support from a speech and language therapist in order to develop their communication skills, and some schools have dedicated speech and language units on site in order to support pupils. Examples of some speech and language problems are given below.

Developmental language disorder

Developmental language disorder (DLD) relates to challenges in understanding or speaking and is a hidden disability. According to Speech and Language UK, around 1.4 million children in the UK have long-term speech, language and communication needs that they won't grow out of. DLD affects around 7.6% of children in the UK, which means that in any class of pupils, two or three will have problems with communication. It may affect children's use of grammar, speech sounds, working memory and overall use of language. There is some evidence to suggest that DLD commonly occurs with ADHD and dyslexia, and that autistic pupils are also more likely to have a developmental language disorder due to links with social communication (Bishop, 2008).

Speech and language delays or disorders

These may range from a stammer to more complex language disorders where pupils have difficulties in thinking through what they want to say. They may have problems with their receptive language skills, which affects their level of understanding, or their expressive language skills, which affects their ability to communicate their thoughts and feelings.

Isolated speech and language feature

This means that the pupil's speech and language has been affected by a physical feature which limits the child or young person's ability to produce clear speech. It may be the only special educational need which the child has.

In addition to this, the communication abilities of pupils who have other areas of special educational need such as cognition and learning, or sensory needs, may be affected by an overriding condition. For example, a child or young person who has learning difficulties may have slower language processing skills or find it difficult to follow instructions. They might also have a limited understanding of non-verbal communication such as facial expressions or body language shown by others. Difficulties with speech, language and communication can also mean that pupils go on to have reading difficulties.

Brilliant example

Myah is working in a Reception class and has been asked to carry out some simple language assessments on the children during their first few weeks of school. She has found that several of the children have skills which are not in line with their age and stage of development. The class teacher will then be able to work with the SENDCo to put some support in place for this group of pupils.

Cognition and learning

Specific cognition and learning difficulties (SpLD) may include dyslexia, dyspraxia or dyscalculia, and as a result pupils may take longer to do their work and need adaptations to be made in order to complete it. Pupils who have cognition and learning needs may find it difficult to absorb new information in the same environments and at the same pace as other pupils, and their needs may be general or specific. For effective learning to take place, pupils need to have developed a range of cognitive skills for processing and storing information. When they have difficulties in this area, there will be an impact on the development of these skills. Pupils may therefore need help in the following areas.

Language, memory and reasoning skills

Children who have cognition and learning difficulties may take longer to develop language skills. This in turn may affect their learning, as they are less able to store and process information.

Sequencing and organisational skills

Some pupils who have SEND may need help and support when organising themselves because they may find it difficult to follow sequences of ideas. For example, they may find it difficult to follow instructions and therefore be unable to carry them out.

Understanding of numbers

The abstract concepts of arithmetic may be difficult for these pupils to grasp and they will need practical help with numbers and to support the development of abstract thought.

Problem solving and concept development

Understanding new ideas and relating them to what they already know may take more time for these pupils and they may need one-to-one support.

Behaviour, social and emotional development

Pupils who have behaviour, social and emotional development needs may display more extreme fluctuations in their behaviour and their needs can be varied, as the reasons for different behaviours are complex. They may demonstrate behaviour relating to mental health conditions such as anxiety, depression, self-harm or eating disorders. As a teaching assistant you may be in a position to gain pupils' trust, and as far as possible, pupils should be encouraged to talk through reasons for their behaviour so that they can be supported effectively. Along with the SENDCo and other professionals, teaching assistants may be able to offer the support that is needed. In some cases, when pupils need long-term emotional support, this may be provided through an Emotional Literacy Support Assistant (ELSA). ELSAs are teaching assistants who have undertaken a specific recognised training course which encompasses social skills, managing emotions, bereavement, anger management and counselling skills.

When managing pupils who have social and emotional needs you will also need to be proactive rather than reactive in your approach – in other words, it is important that pupils are also aware of guidelines for their behaviour and the consequences of their actions. They need to be given opportunities to develop relationships with others and treat them with respect. If you are working with these pupils as an individual support assistant you will need to work closely with other professionals to decide on the best form of intervention to use, but developing a positive relationship and finding out as much as possible about them is a good starting point. As well as their EHCP, these pupils may also be given a Behaviour Support Plan (BSP) if they need to have shorter-term targets for more regular review. (For more on behaviour management in general, see Chapter 5.)

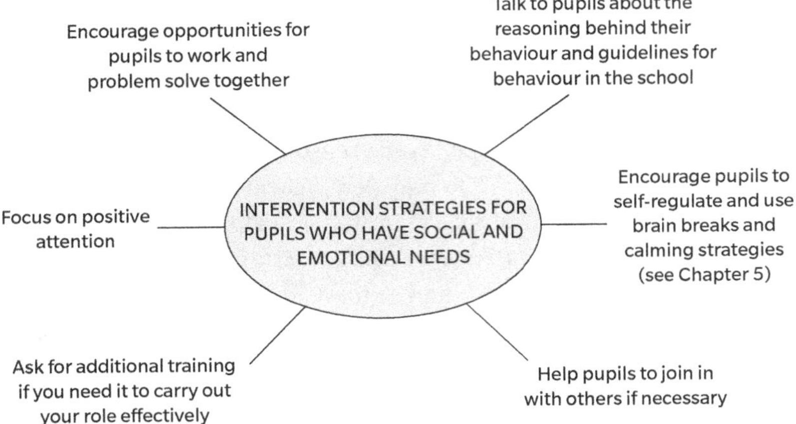

Figure 6.2 Strategies for behaviour intervention

> ## Brilliant tip
>
> What works as a great behaviour management strategy one week may not work on another – you will need to vary the strategies you use so have plenty ready to use, particularly with younger children.

Sensory and/or physical

Pupils with sensory and/or physical development needs will require support in the areas of hearing, visual or physical conditions. They may have a disability or medical condition which impacts on all areas of their learning, or they may need very little support, which may change over time. It should not be assumed that these pupils need any form of special educational provision if they are able to access the curriculum without support, as their condition may not impact on their educational needs. However, in some cases, pupils will require specialised provision to ensure that they are included in all areas of the curriculum. Depending on their needs, you should find out about any specialist equipment which they have and be able to select and use any materials required to support their learning. Pupils with sensory or physical impairments may tire easily and their social and emotional development may be affected as they may become frustrated if they are not able to complete tasks as quickly or as well as they would hope to.

You should ensure that pupils with disabilities are encouraged to participate as much as possible in all activities alongside their peers and that you only intervene if necessary and after speaking to the pupil.

Brilliant dos and don'ts

Do

- ✔ Develop a good (but professional!) relationship with the pupil through getting to know them and their parents or carers.
- ✔ Ask your SENDCo if you can read any paperwork relating to the pupil and for a copy of their BSP or EHCP; however, remember that this information is confidential.
- ✔ Always keep an eye out for any resources which may be useful.

Don't

- ✗ Have stereotypical views of pupils or their families.
- ✗ Try to take over or do work for pupils.
- ✗ Become personally involved with pupils and their families.

Working with pupils in intervention groups

Teaching assistants are often asked to work with groups of pupils to raise their attainment in a specific subject area following regular assessments of their progress. Most often these interventions will be in social or communication skills, English or maths, or will focus on supporting pupils' mental health. The teacher should provide a programme of work or series of sessions, which is usually worked on daily or several times a week by a teaching assistant. This will focus on pupils' particular areas of need and develop their knowledge as well as consolidating their skills. The pupils will be monitored throughout the programme and their progress will be reviewed at the end of a set number of sessions. Teachers and teaching assistants will then discuss whether they need to continue or if they have made sufficient progress to be able to stop the intervention.

Brilliant case study

Ryan has been asked to work with three boys in Years 3 and 4 who have recently been diagnosed with autism to support their social and communication skills. He has been asked to take the group out twice a week but has not been given very much guidance from the SENDCo as to make best use of his time. Although he has some experience, he is finding it challenging to manage the group due to the boys' behaviour and his own lack of confidence.

- What should Ryan do?
- How can he best support the boys so that they get the most out of the sessions?

Working with your SENDCo and understanding their role

If you are working with pupils who have special educational needs it is likely that you will be managed by or have a close relationship with your SENDCo. The SENDCo is responsible for the day-to-day co-ordination of educational provision for pupils in the school with special educational needs and disabilities. They will usually be a member of the school's senior management team although this is not always the case. It is likely that they will have a large workload as they will be responsible for managing the paperwork not only for pupils with EHCPs but also all intervention programmes in the school and all pupils who have additional support and BSPs. As well as advising other school staff, they will also need to co-ordinate the advice and reports written by external professionals, as well as managing appointments between these professionals along with parents or carers and teaching staff. In some cases, the SENDCo will also be the line manager for teaching assistants in the school and so may carry out appraisals and arrange their continuing professional development (for more on this, see Chapter 10).

Requirements for the role of the SENDCo are that they should have a teaching qualification as well as a specific qualification if they have been appointed from 2014 onwards. This is the National Award for Special Educational Needs Co-ordination and should be awarded within three years of being in their post if this is in a mainstream school.

You should have time set aside with the SENDCo to discuss any issues which come up in your work with pupils. This may mean going through new reports or strategies which have been suggested by other professionals, so that you can work out how to fit these in to the pupil's timetable, and also to discuss any issues both before and after any meetings with parents or carers as well as external agencies. The school may also have a SENDCo assistant, who should have some time set aside to provide support with administration and the development of resources and co-ordinating support. It is important that the assistant and SENDCo also have some time together each week to discuss issues and catch up.

Brilliant case study

You are working as an individual support assistant for Bhumika, who is in Year 5. She is autistic and also has problems with social communication. The autism advisory teacher comes into school once a term to observe Bhumika and to speak to you, and then separately to Bhumika's parents and the SENDCo. He writes a report which gives suggested targets for Bhumika's EHCP, which he goes through with you and always tells you that you will have a copy. However, in the eighteen months you have been at the school you have never received a copy. You have asked the SENDCo several times and although she always says that she will pass it on to you this has not happened. You can only assume that this is because she is always so busy.

- Why is it important that you should get to see the report?
- What would you do in this situation?

Working with parents and carers

The SEND Code of Practice was introduced in 2014 and made significant changes to the previous version regarding the process of identifying, assessing and supporting pupils with special educational needs. It focuses more on the participation of children and young people and their parents or carers in the decisions which are made around their progress. As a result, if you are working 1:1 with a pupil who has special educational needs or disabilities, you should find that you are working closely both with pupils and families as part of your role.

The most important area to remember when working with parents or carers is that lines of communication will need to be kept open at all times. You will need to establish a positive relationship with them in order to ensure that the flow of information between home and school is continuous. The relationship should be one of mutual support and co-operation as both the school and parents or carers will have the pupil's interests at the heart of all they do. It is also important to involve them with all assessments and reviews so that as much information as possible is gathered about the pupil. The school will need to make sure that parents or carers have regular information about the pupil's progress, are aware of any intervention which is made, and are encouraged to contribute in any way which may support their child. Schools will also need to consult them before referring the pupil to any other professional. The school should also ensure that they are as supportive as possible to parents or carers, who may be under pressure due to their child's needs, and respect their contributions and points of view. All schools should have a member of staff who is a family support worker, and if you are supporting an individual pupil you may need to work alongside this staff member.

The role of family support workers

The family support worker was originally only accessed through social worker and counselling services. However, due to the extended schools agenda, education family support workers have developed in recent years to form a school-based, closer and more productive link between schools and families. Family support workers are often allocated some time within their day to spend talking to parents or carers and families, and developing closer links where these are needed. They support parents or carers and pupils and can provide an informal but often much needed ear which can be perceived as less intimidating than speaking to a member of teaching staff. Family support workers will also liaise with parents or carers to develop additional extended school provision where this is needed or to advise and support them if further services are required. In many cases they will work with parents or carers to support pupils who are having difficulties at school and try to enable them to overcome any barriers which they are facing.

If you are working as a family support worker as part of your role within school, you should have been offered additional training and support. The role can often be similar to that of a counsellor and you will need to be a good listener as well as being able to relate well to others. If you have additional skills such as speaking a second language, especially if it is one spoken by large numbers of parents or carers, this will be particularly useful. You will need to be available at the beginning and end of the day when parents or carers may be on site although they should also be able to make appointments to see you if they need more time.

Brilliant tip

If you are working as a family support worker, make sure that your school newsletter or website regularly reminds families that you are there, or that the school noticeboard gives this information – it is often the case that parents and carers will not remember that you are there until they need you.

All local authorities will also have a Parent Partnership Service, which will provide advice and information to parents or carers of children and young people who have special educational needs and disabilities.

Brilliant activity

Find out more about your local Parent Partnership Service and the information which it provides to parents or carers.

Working with outside agencies

There are a number of different agencies with whom you may come into contact when working with pupils who have special educational needs and disabilities. These will mainly be based outside school and pupils will usually have appointments during or after lessons. However, they may also act in an advisory role and come to the school to give support for strategies which may be used when working with pupils who have special educational needs and disabilities. If you are starting to work with an individual pupil, you will need to find out those agencies who are working with the pupil and whether you need to be present at any meetings which take place. The main agencies with whom you may come into contact will be the following:

Speech and language therapist

The speech and language therapist (SALT) will give support to pupils with a range of communication difficulties. The pupil will need to be referred to the speech therapist either through their GP or the school and will usually be given six-week 'blocks' of therapy as well as work for pupils and families to do at home and advice for the school. The SENDCo will also liaise with the SALT to continue work in school on a day-to-day basis until the next block of therapy.

Occupational therapist

The occupational therapist will work with pupils on programmes to develop their fine motor skills. These are to do with the level of control they have over their hands, for example cutting, threading, fastenings, and pen and pencil control. They will develop individual programmes for pupils to use at home, as well as giving advice for activities that they can work on at school.

Physiotherapist

The physiotherapist will work with pupils on programmes to develop their gross motor skills. These are to do with the level of control they have over their arms and legs, for example walking, running, jumping, waving, throwing and so on. They will develop individual programmes for pupils to use at home, as well as giving advice for activities that they can work on at school.

Children and Young People's Mental Health Services (CYPMHS)

Also known as CAMHS or Child and Adolescent Mental Health Services, these professionals work with all children and young people who need support with their mental health. They are usually NHS funded although some may be from other sectors, and children may be referred to them through schools or GPs.

Educational psychologist

The educational psychologist will come in and work with the school to assess pupils who are a cause for concern and to decide whether it is appropriate for them to go for a statutory assessment. Often the educational psychologist will work long term with specific pupils if the school has concerns and will meet with parents or carers and school staff to devise learning plans and will write reports.

Sensory support teacher

When a school starts working with a pupil who has sensory support needs, the sensory support teacher will come into school to advise staff how to prepare the learning environment and give advice about managing their needs. For example, the school may need advice and/or equipment if they have a pupil with a hearing or visual impairment.

Autism advisory teacher

This teacher will be a specialist in working with pupils who have autistic spectrum disorder and may occasionally come to school to observe and devise specific strategies for individuals. If you are working with a pupil with autism, you may have some contact with this teacher.

> **Brilliant tip**
>
> Make sure you know about any external professionals who work with individual pupils you support. If they write reports or advice for the school, your SENDCo should give you a copy.

Working in a special school

Special schools exist as provision for pupils whose needs cannot be met in a mainstream school. They may specialise in specific conditions or needs, such as pupil behaviour, or may be for pupils who have moderate, severe or profound learning difficulties. If you are working in a special school, it is likely that your role will vary from day to day depending on the needs of the children. In some special schools, all support staff will support all pupils, as there will be fewer numbers and all staff will know all pupils, whilst in others you may support a named pupil. In all cases, you will need to know where to find the pupils' EHCPs and find out as much as you can about their needs so that you can support them effectively. You may be given a different timetable depending on the day and who is available, or you may have the same routine each day. You may also need to have additional training depending on the school and the needs of the pupils, for example if you are working with pupils who have severe or profound needs. You may also be required to carry out lifting or be asked to work on specific physio or occupational therapy with pupils, and need training in the use of equipment. In some cases, you may also need to adapt equipment and resources for the pupils you support.

Depending on the school, you may not have as much contact with parents or carers as at a mainstream school, as in some special schools the pupils will arrive and leave each day in special transport buses. However, parents or carers will be encouraged to participate in the life of the school in other ways and they should be in regular contact with them.

Brilliant recap

- Make sure you know all you can about the needs of the pupil or pupils you support.
- Work with parents or carers and involve them in their child's progress.
- Be sensitive to the needs of pupils and their families.
- Make sure you go for any training that is available on the pupil's needs or condition.
- Be aware of work with any external professionals who are involved with the pupil.
- Work closely with your SENDCo and talk to others who may have worked with the pupil.

Further reading

Bishop, Dorothy V. M. (2008) Specific language impairment, dyslexia, and autism: Using genetics to unravel their relationship. In C. F. Norbury, J. B. Tomblin & D. V. M. Bishop (Eds.), *Understanding developmental language disorders: from theory to practice* (pp. 67–78). Hove: Psychology Press.

Conkbayir, Mine (2023) *The Neuroscience of the Developing Child*, Routledge.

Dix, Paul (2009) *Taking Care of Behaviour*, Pearson.

Sobel, Daniel and Alston, Sara (2021) *The Inclusive Classroom*, Bloomsbury.

Teaching and Supporting Children with SEND in Primary Schools, 3rd edition (2019) Sage Publications.

There are a large number of websites which may be useful, and in the first instance you should ask your SENDCo for information which is relevant to your needs. However if you are supporting a pupil who has specific needs it is worth finding out whether there is a society or support group who can provide help and advice.

www.nasen.org.uk – National Association for Special Educational Needs

www.senmagazine.co.uk – free magazine for all those who work with pupils who have SEND.

The Communication Trust: www.speechandlanguage.org.uk – resources and interventions to support speech, language and communication.

www.elsanetwork.org – website providing contacts and information for ELSAs

www.bdadyslexia.org.uk – British Dyslexia Association

www.csie.org.uk – Centre for Studies on Inclusive Education

Chapter 7

Diversity, equity and inclusion

All adults working in schools will need to be aware of the importance of promoting equity,* diversity and inclusion in their work with pupils. Those from all backgrounds should be respected and have full access to all aspects of school life as well as the curriculum, and all staff and pupils should be protected from abuse and discrimination. This chapter will also look at how teaching assistants can support pupils who speak English as an additional language, including strategies for promoting pupils' language development in speaking and listening, reading and writing in English.

* The term equality may also be used in this context. You should be aware, however, that there is a difference between the two terms:

- **Equality:** ensuring that the same resources and opportunities are provided to everyone.
- **Equity**: providing the resources and opportunities which are needed in order to make things fair. In this context, it may mean that some pupils have more help than others due to their circumstances or educational needs.

Relevant legislation

As a teaching assistant, you will need to know about legislation and requirements for equity and diversity in schools so that you can apply it to your work with children and young people. There are a number of regulations and codes of practice which are relevant to equity, diversity and human rights.

The Equality Act 2010

This is the most important legislation for equity and diversity in England. It aims to protect the rights of individuals so that everyone is given fair treatment and is not discriminated against. It applies to all schools in the UK as well as wider society.

The Equality Act legally protects people from discrimination related to nine protected characteristics (see Table 7.1), and schools will be inspected with this in mind. There are some exceptions in the case of schools, however, which are included in the table below together with examples and applicability.

Table 7.1 The nine protected characteristics under the Equality Act 2010

Protected characteristic	What this might mean in school
Sex	This means that children and young people should not be discriminated against due to their gender and that the curriculum and other school-based activities should be available to all. However, schools *are* allowed to discriminate against pupils because of their gender when admitting pupils if they are a single-sex school.
Sexual orientation	Pupils should not be discriminated against due to their sexual orientation. An example of this might be if pupils are excluded from activities or bullied due to their sexual orientation. They should also be given age-appropriate relationships education or RSE as part of the curriculum.

Protected characteristic	What this might mean in school
Religion/belief	A pupil's religion or belief should not be a cause for discrimination. However, an exception to this is in the case of a non-profit-making religious organisation such as a faith school which is for pupils of a specific religion. They may wish to restrict admission to pupils of a faith or religion and this should be set out in their aims or ethos. An example of this might be a Christian school which may discriminate against a pupil of a different religion in favour of offering a place to a Christian child.
Race or ethnicity	This means that pupils should not be excluded from schools or from activities due to their race or ethnicity, or for any other reason. Any bullying or anti-social behaviour should be immediately addressed in line with the school's anti-bullying and behaviour policies.
Pregnancy/ maternity	This will be relevant to pupils in secondary schools. Pupils should not be discriminated against or treated unfavourably in the case of pregnancy or maternity and should be given the same opportunities as others. An example of this might be if a school says that a pupil may not return to school or college after having a baby. All young people are required to stay in full-time education until they are 18.
Marriage/civil partnership	This protected characteristic is unlikely to be referred to for pupils in schools in England and Wales, as the legal age for marriage and civil partnerships has been 18 since February 2023.
Gender reassignment	Although the permitted age for gender reassignment is 17 in England and 18 in Wales, pupils may have questions or concerns about their gender from an earlier age and need some support. Schools may be involved in working with pupils and parents or carers and there may be some discussion with healthcare or other professionals. An example of this may be a pupil who wants to go onto hormonal treatment such as puberty blockers and approaches the school for advice.

Table 7.1 continued

Protected characteristic	What this might mean in school
Disability	Disabled pupils should have access to the same opportunities as their peers. Schools are required to make 'reasonable adjustments' in order to remove any barriers which exist to the inclusion of all pupils. An example of discrimination might be if a school does not adapt the learning environment to provide access for a wheelchair user.
Age	Pupils in school should undertake age-appropriate activities but it is not illegal for schools to discriminate due to age. For example, pupils in England start school in the academic year that they are 5 years old.

You can read guidance to the Equality Act at www.gov.uk/ (search for equality-act-2010-guidance and click on the tab Equality Act 2010: guidance).

United Nations Convention on the Rights of the Child (UNCRC) 1989

This is an international and legally binding agreement signed by the UK along with 195 other states. It states that all children and young people have the right to survival, protection and education – whatever their background, language, ability, gender, religion or ethnicity. It sets out their rights in the form of 54 articles stating how they should be treated equally and without discrimination. Those which are the most relevant to schools include Articles 2, 3, 6 and 12 (see Table 7.2). You can read the full text at www.unicef.org/ (in the tab Research and Reports, under the head Child rights and global goals check for Convention on the Rights of the Child).

Table 7.2 A brief description of the four articles of the UNCRC which are relevant to schools.

Article 2	The UNCRC applies to every child whatever their ability, status or background.
Article 3	The child's best interests should always be a priority.
Article 6	Every child has the right to life.
Article 12	Every child has the right to be heard and express their views and wishes.

Special Educational Needs Code of Practice 2014

The SEND Code of practice sets out how local authorities, health bodies, schools and colleges should ensure the inclusion of children and young people with special educational needs and disabilities up to the age of 25. It is statutory, which means that all schools must follow it. Your school will also have a SEND Policy which will set out how they meet local and national requirements. You can read the full text of the Code of Practice at www.gov.uk/ (in the search bar, look for SEND code of practice: 0 to 25 years). (For more on working with pupils who have SEND, see Chapter 6.)

Understanding discrimination

Discrimination relates to treating a person with a protected characteristic in a way which is less favourable than the way we treat others. For example, this may be a pupil who has a hearing impairment and is not provided with a hearing loop or additional resources to give them the same access to learning as other pupils. All adults working in schools should be aware that there are different types of discrimination:

- **Direct discrimination** is clear and means treating one person differently from another because of one or more of the nine protected characteristics as above (e.g. the hearing-impaired pupil).

- **Indirect discrimination** may be harder to identify. It means applying a rule which may affect some people more than others. For example, having a uniform policy which may affect Muslim pupils more because the policy does not allow them to wear a head covering.
- **Harassment** means the use of offensive behaviour towards an individual which relates to a protected characteristic, for example bullying a person from a different ethnic group or because of their sexual orientation.
- **Victimisation** relates to poor or unfair treatment if a person has complained about discrimination or harassment, for example a pregnant pupil not being given support to continue with their studies.

We are all a product of our own backgrounds and experiences, and may not realise that the way in which we are treating others is discriminatory. The resulting subconscious attitudes or opinions are known as implicit or unconscious bias and may lead to indirect discrimination.

Brilliant example

Jaki is a teaching assistant in a primary school in Year 1 which has a high turnover of pupils from a Gypsy, Roma and Traveller background. She has been asked to work with a group of pupils and notices that one of them is showing particular skill in the area of mathematical calculation. She decides not to say anything to the teacher as she feels that the pupil is only five years old and is likely to move on soon.

Brilliant case study

A primary school is sending Year 6 on a residential trip at the end of the year to an outdoor activity centre, which they do every year. There are two pupils who have disabilities in the year group who they have now realised will be excluded from the trip as the school has not taken their needs into consideration.

- What kind of discrimination is this?
- How could the school and/or the centre make a reasonable adjustment so that the pupils can take part?

Pupils can also discriminate against one another and may harass or victimise other pupils causing emotional distress and abuse. This may involve a range of behaviours, from name calling to online trolling. The school's Equality and Diversity, Bullying, Behaviour and E safety policies are a starting point for staff when working with pupils and parents or carers to deal with any discriminatory behaviour. It is also likely that senior management will be involved due to the seriousness of this kind of behaviour.

Equality and diversity policy

Your school should have an up-to-date equality/equity and diversity policy which will set out how it aims to meet legal requirements in relation to equity of opportunity. As in the case of all legislation, you will need to check from time to time to make sure that what is being used is still current. The school's equality and diversity policy should also look at the way in which the school protects pupils from any type of abuse, discrimination or bullying and make sure that all staff know how to:

- respond to any behaviours that are not in line with the policy
- ensure that activities, resources and facilities in the learning environment are accessible to all pupils
- ensure that teaching in the school promotes multiculturalism and diversity

The policy should set out the steps which the school will take when they are made aware of this type of treatment. It may also link to other school policies such as the cyberbullying policy which aims to prevent online bullying, the school's behaviour policy or staff whistleblowing policy.

Brilliant activity

Find a copy of your school's equality and diversity policy. What kinds of examples can you find of the ways in which the school values and promotes cultural diversity and what is your role in this? What does your school do when it is made aware of abuse or bullying?

Promoting equity, diversity and inclusion

Promoting equity, diversity and inclusion means ensuring that you value and respect pupils from a range of backgrounds and cultures. Pupils in the school should develop an awareness of the value of diversity in society as well as being able to develop a positive sense of their own identity. Schools will usually have measures in place through the school's equality and diversity policy to ensure that the whole school community recognises and celebrates a variety of religious and cultural festivals through assemblies, visitors and trips, and encourages pupils to find out about other languages and faiths through religious and personal, social and health education (PSHE). Resources and displays around the school should also include representation from different backgrounds and cultures. All adults will need to act as role models and treat others with respect so that pupils are given positive examples of behaviour towards others. The school should also encourage the involvement of all parents or carers in the life of the school as much as possible; this is important both to encourage communication and to ensure that pupils feel that the school and families value one another.

Brilliant activity

Errison works in an inner city primary school and is doing his level 2 qualification in supporting teaching and learning. He has been asked to move around the school or explore the school website and note down examples of the way in which the school shows that it celebrates diversity. So far he has found welcome notices in the entrance hall in different languages, a range of books in the library which represent different cultures, races and religions, and a Chinese New Year display in the corridor. He has also found examples on the website of events such as open evenings for speakers of other languages.

- Go for a walk around in your school and see how many visual examples of diversity you can find.
- What other ways does your school celebrate diversity and inclusion?

In order to ensure that we treat all pupils with equity, we need to look at our own views and attitudes to ensure that we are not stereotyping others or using unconscious bias to make judgements about what they can and cannot do. Schools may offer training on unconscious or implicit bias, which relates to attitudes that may influence and affect our decisions. We may generalise about groups of people based on our experiences but also through what we see in the media and wider society. Unconscious bias is the way in which we can be influenced by shared characteristics with others or those which we are more familiar with, and this may impact pupils in a negative way. For example, if you are working with a group which includes a pupil with a disability and make an assumption that they will not be able to complete a task without giving them the opportunity to, you may be preventing them from achieving their potential. Stereotyping is another form of unconscious bias, for example we may assume that all boys will be good at sport or that all girls will have a caring nature. You may also need to encourage those who do not think they are capable of achieving a particular activity.

Brilliant activity

Research the use and impact of stereotyping in schools. How does the media influence how different groups of people are portrayed?

Brilliant case study

A class of Year 7 children have been asked to carry out a PE activity which they have not done before in which they have to run along a track and jump over a series of hurdles at a new local sports centre. The pupils are mainly keen although four of them think that they will not be able to do it and are saying that it would be better if they cheered the others on. As the teaching assistant, you have been asked to speak to the pupils who are lacking confidence to encourage them to have a go. You persuade them and to their surprise, one of them comes first.

- Why is it important to give all pupils the same opportunities?
- What might you have said to those who did not want to carry out the activity?

Pupils who speak English as an additional language (EAL)

According to government statistics in 2023, 20.2% of pupils in British schools were recorded as having a first language other than English. In schools, children will need to know that their culture and status are valued as this will help them to feel settled and secure, factors which will contribute to their being able to develop skills in a new language. If they are feeling isolated or anxious, it is more likely that this will be difficult for them.

Many teaching assistants support these pupils either as an English/Welsh speaker or as a bilingual assistant – that is, speaking to pupils in their own language in order to help them to access the curriculum. If you support bilingual or multilingual pupils, you will need to have an awareness of the way in which children process language and the importance for bilingual pupils of retaining their identity through valuing their home culture and language. As well as pupils speaking a second language, you should also think about how aspects of culture, religion, home and family circumstances and upbringing can affect their learning.

The process of language development

So that we can build a picture of how we learn language, it is important to think about the two stages which linguists consider that all children pass through. These are known as the pre-linguistic and the linguistic stages.

The pre-linguistic stage is during the first twelve months, when babies begin to learn the skills of basic communication. During this time, they will start to attract the attention of adults and repeat back the different sounds they hear. This is true of any language, but although babies worldwide are born with the potential to make the same sounds, by the age of twelve months they can only repeat back the sounds that they have heard around them during that time. In the case of deaf babies who cannot hear the sounds around them, developmental timeframes for language will be different.

Brilliant tip

You should be aware that when learning a new language, it is normal to have a 'silent phase' when the learner is 'tuning in' to new sounds and vocabulary, in the same way that a baby does when learning one language. Try not to push learners into speaking English until they are ready.

The linguistic stage is when babies start to use the words that they hear and learn how to put sentences together. Children will develop this stage gradually over the next few years so that by the age of about five years they are fluent in their home language. For children who are learning more than one language from the earliest stages however, learning to speak may be slightly slower as they will need to absorb different language systems.

If children have learned two or more languages simultaneously from an early age and they have been able to listen to good language models, it is likely that they will be confident in them and be able to 'switch' languages. When learning two languages together, children will need to be able to tune in to the language with the person who is speaking to them – in this way it will be easier for them to distinguish between the different languages. Problems may arise however if one parent, for example, regularly switches languages in the early stages of learning language, as the child will find it difficult to know which language they are listening to at any given time. Once languages are established and the child grows older and more confident this will be less important.

Brilliant case study

You are working in a Reception class and Irena has started school alongside other children. Her parents are Latvian and she speaks Latvian at home with her family so her English has been learned at Nursery and from the TV. As a result, Irena's English is less well developed than her Latvian although she does speak both languages. Her mother asks you and the class teacher for advice to encourage Irena to develop her spoken English.

- What should you say to Irena's mother?
- How could you support Irena in developing her spoken English?

As an adult working in an educational setting, the most important thing for you to be aware of is the importance of language development as a route to learning. Language is the basis for the way in which we organise our thoughts, ideas and feelings. We need to support all children to develop language skills and to build on their knowledge so that they are more able to access the curriculum.

Finding out about the pupil's background

If you are working with bilingual pupils or others from a different cultural background who are new to your school, you will need to find out as much as you can about their home and educational background and circumstances so that you can support them more effectively. Schools may do this in different ways:

Background forms

The school will have a system for gathering initial information from parents or carers through forms. These will usually request basic information, medical details, child's position in the family, previous schools and languages spoken.

Home visits

Depending on your school and the age of the pupil, a home visit may be carried out to find out more about the pupil and their home background. If the pupil's parents or carers do not speak any English, the school may decide to invite them to school with an interpreter so that they can speak to them more directly. In many cases, schools may use translation programmes on computers to help them with communication.

Records from previous schools

If the pupil has been to school in the UK before, their previous school will be asked to send transfer records and information about their progress, including their ability in the target language. They may also contain records from other agencies if these have been involved in working with the pupil, such as speech therapists.

However, although some information may arrive electronically, be aware that some material may take some time to arrive and may not be at your school before the pupil starts. Your SENDCo or teachers may need to call the previous school and speak to staff there if necessary in order to gather information.

Once you have gathered initial information on the pupil you will have a clearer idea about their needs and be able to work with teachers to devise how they should be assessed and their needs met.

Brilliant case study

Bohdan came to the UK from Ukraine at the start of the war. He has been in the UK for two years but has had to switch schools due to a house move. He has just arrived in your school in Year 8 and is not speaking at all, although it is clear he understands most of what is being said. Your school has not yet received any records from his previous school.

- What could be done to find out more about Bohdan's situation?
- How can the school develop more of an idea of his language needs?

The role of self-esteem in developing communication

It is helpful if all staff are made aware if a pupil who is new to the school does not speak English. In the case of teaching assistants in primary schools this will usually be the class teacher, whilst in secondary schools it may be the SENDCo. This is because, as well as feeling that they fit in, pupils' self-esteem and confidence may be affected by their perception of how others see them. It is especially important for everyone to know and pronounce their name correctly. If their parents or carers do not speak English, this may be a pupil's first experience of having to communicate with others in a language other than their own. It is important for the pupil to be able to communicate in school, and although they will usually pick up a new language reasonably quickly, this can be a difficult time for them and you should be sensitive to this. If you notice that a pupil is having problems it is important to discuss this with teachers, as there will be strategies that you can put in place to support them.

Brilliant example

Spend time with the pupil at break times and encourage them to socialise with others through playground games with younger children, or give them a buddy or assign someone that they can go to if they need to find something out or are unsure of what to do.

Brilliant case study

Sobiga is a new pupil in your class who does not speak any English. Although she has made friends and is involved in class activities, you have noticed that at breaktimes and lunchtimes she is often on her own.

- What kind of support does Sobiga need and why?
- List some strategies that you could use to help her to develop her confidence and language skills.

How to support the language skills of bilingual and multilingual pupils

Although pupil learning in general may be affected by their background and you will need to know about this and be sensitive to it (see also Chapter 3 for factors affecting learning), your focus when working with bilingual pupils will be on the development of their language. You may be working with individuals or groups of pupils to help them with their speaking and listening, reading or writing. Although the approach you take with very young children may be different from that you use with older pupils, the strategies you use should be similar and should apply across the curriculum.

Your initial work with pupils should be based on an assessment of their level of language as well as their level of ability. You should have guidance and support either from your SENDCo or from teachers, but this will be the starting point for any individual work or targets which are devised for the pupil, who may be at different stages in their development of English. Remember that a pupil's ability to speak another language does not necessarily mean that they have a special educational need. The SENDCo may be involved in devising educational plans for pupils who are at the earliest stages of learning English as an additional language; it is important that their progress is monitored and that they settle into school. However, although at the initial stages of learning a language these pupils may need extra support, learning a second language is not an indicator of either higher or lower ability.

Speaking and listening skills

As in all learning situations, the effective use of praise is very important when working with pupils who speak English as an additional language. You need to provide encouragement and support to these pupils as they will be insecure about the way in which they use their second language. Figure 7.1 shows other strategies you will need to use.

Brilliant dos and don'ts

Do

- ✔ Involve bilingual pupils in purposeful talk as much as possible.
- ✔ Allow pupils more thinking time to prepare for what they want to say.
- ✔ Model correct use of language for them rather than correcting them.
- ✔ Give visual examples where possible.

Don't

- ✗ Answer questions for bilingual pupils.
- ✗ Put pupils who speak additional languages in groups with lower ability pupils, or group them all together.
- ✗ Ask pupils to 'say something' in their language to demonstrate to others that they speak another language, unless there is a purpose to their doing it.

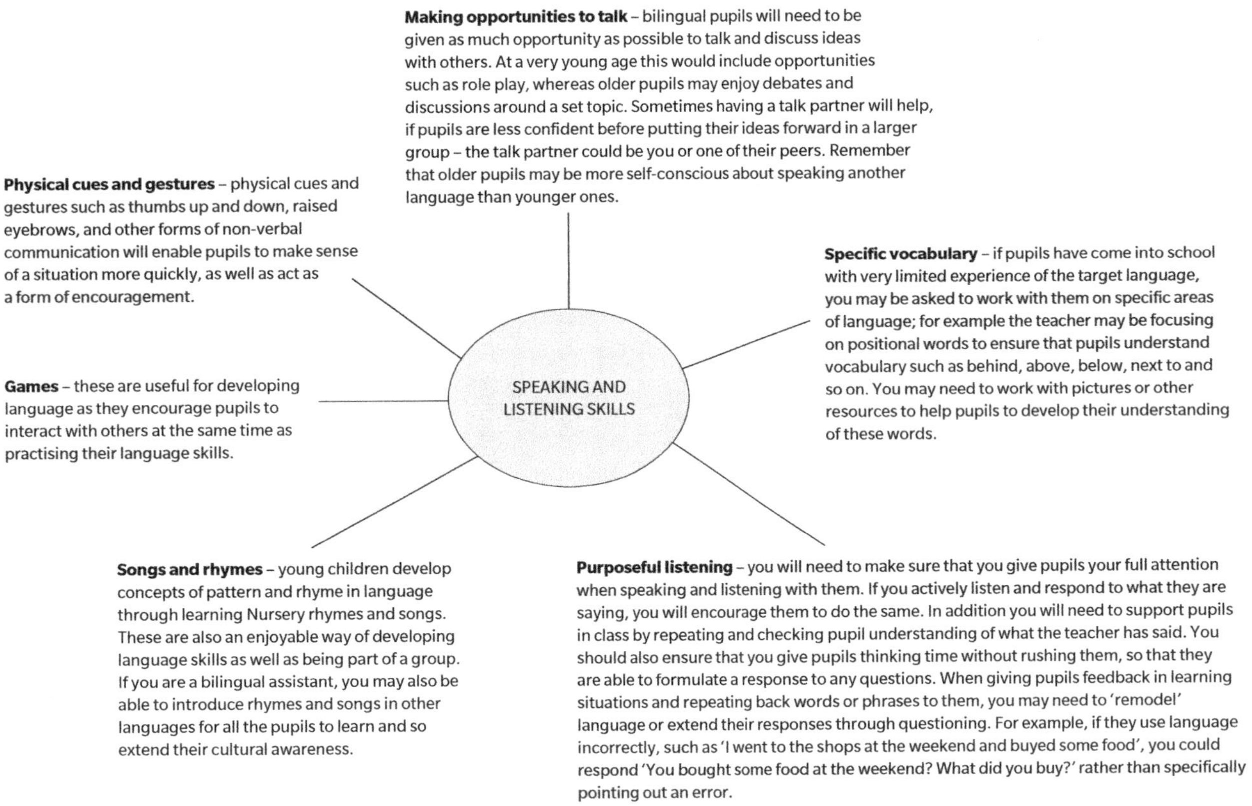

SPEAKING AND LISTENING SKILLS

Making opportunities to talk – bilingual pupils will need to be given as much opportunity as possible to talk and discuss ideas with others. At a very young age this would include opportunities such as role play, whereas older pupils may enjoy debates and discussions around a set topic. Sometimes having a talk partner will help, if pupils are less confident before putting their ideas forward in a larger group – the talk partner could be you or one of their peers. Remember that older pupils may be more self-conscious about speaking another language than younger ones.

Specific vocabulary – if pupils have come into school with very limited experience of the target language, you may be asked to work with them on specific areas of language; for example the teacher may be focusing on positional words to ensure that pupils understand vocabulary such as behind, above, below, next to and so on. You may need to work with pictures or other resources to help pupils to develop their understanding of these words.

Purposeful listening – you will need to make sure that you give pupils your full attention when speaking and listening with them. If you actively listen and respond to what they are saying, you will encourage them to do the same. In addition you will need to support pupils in class by repeating and checking pupil understanding of what the teacher has said. You should also ensure that you give pupils thinking time without rushing them, so that they are able to formulate a response to any questions. When giving pupils feedback in learning situations and repeating back words or phrases to them, you may need to 'remodel' language or extend their responses through questioning. For example, if they use language incorrectly, such as 'I went to the shops at the weekend and buyed some food', you could respond 'You bought some food at the weekend? What did you buy?' rather than specifically pointing out an error.

Songs and rhymes – young children develop concepts of pattern and rhyme in language through learning Nursery rhymes and songs. These are also an enjoyable way of developing language skills as well as being part of a group. If you are a bilingual assistant, you may also be able to introduce rhymes and songs in other languages for all the pupils to learn and so extend their cultural awareness.

Games – these are useful for developing language as they encourage pupils to interact with others at the same time as practising their language skills.

Physical cues and gestures – physical cues and gestures such as thumbs up and down, raised eyebrows, and other forms of non-verbal communication will enable pupils to make sense of a situation more quickly, as well as act as a form of encouragement.

Figure 7.1 Suggested strategies for developing speaking and listening skills

You will also need to remember that there is a difference between the social language in which pupils may be starting to become fluent at the earlier stages and 'classroom' language. This is because in social situations the meaning of what is being communicated is often backed up by visual cues. It may also be different to the correct form of written English. Classroom language is likely to be more abstract, particularly in the case of older pupils, and it can be hard for them to tune into the kinds of functional language required in some learning situations, for example hypothesising, evaluating, predicting and inferring. Mathematical language can also be a difficulty if they have not come across some of the terms which are used. It is likely that as pupils get older there will be less visual demonstration to support learning – you will need to be able to give practical support to pupils and continue to check their understanding of what is being asked.

Brilliant example

Jez is working in a Year 6 class with two pupils who speak English as a second language. He has noticed that they are having some difficulty with the work that the class are doing in maths and asks the class teacher if he can check their understanding of what they are being asked to do as well as using some practical examples to help them. He talks through the task with the pupils to make sure they understand and gets out some maths apparatus to help them to work through it.

Reading and writing skills

As you are developing the speaking and listening skills of bilingual pupils, you will also need to be able to find opportunities to support their reading and writing skills in English. Pupils will need to be able to link the development of the spoken word with reading and writing and should participate in all lessons with their peers so that they can observe good practice from other pupils. However, if they need additional focused support, you may need to adapt or modify learning resources that others are using in order to help them to access the curriculum more fully. You may also need to explain and reinforce specific vocabulary if it is part of a topic or subject area. As with all other pupils, they will need to be able to experience a variety of texts, both fiction and non-fiction, in order to maximise their vocabulary.

Brilliant activity

Find out about the different kinds of resources that are available in your school for supporting bilingual pupils. Were they easy to find? What was the source?

Working as a Bilingual Teaching Assistant (BTA)

If you are bilingual yourself, you may have been employed or asked by the school to use pupils' first language to support teaching and learning. You may also be involved in providing support for families and liaising with them in order to promote pupil participation. This role will often be created in schools which have a high percentage of bilingual learners to make it easier for the school to encourage communication between the school and families who do not speak English. If this is your role, you should have some opportunity to work with the governor or named teacher in the school who is responsible for advising teachers about EAL learners. You should also be able to feed back to teachers, in particular if there are concerns about specific pupils. Qualifications are also available for bilingual assistants who work mainly in this role.

Bilingual assistants will often support pupils who have a limited knowledge of English by assessing their ability in their home language. It is helpful to be able to gauge their level of fluency – if this is good it will be easier for them to learn a second language more quickly as they will have another language to relate it to.

If you are working in a school with a high percentage of pupils who speak a particular language, you may support individuals or groups of pupils in order to help them to develop their English skills whilst also speaking to them in their first language. It can also help to detect any language disorder or learning delay which pupils may have as these can take longer to become evident in pupils who speak additional languages. In this situation you will need to refer to your SENDCo or to teachers who will need to refer the pupil for specialist assessment.

Giving feedback to pupils, families and colleagues

As a bilingual assistant it is likely that you will be involved in meetings and discussions with teachers and families about pupil progress. Pupils should also be fully involved in the procedure if possible. The best way in which to do this is to set aside a regular time with pupils and teachers to discuss their progress and to think about any additional support they might need. You may also be invited to parents' evenings and other events in order to support teachers and other staff in passing information on to parents or carers. If you have been asked to do this, you should have some time to speak to teachers beforehand so that you know what information the teachers need to have passed on and how they would like you to structure what you say.

You will also need to be able to give feedback to colleagues, particularly if the pupil speaks very little English. Colleagues will need you to pass on information about pupil development in English and also their knowledge and use of their home language, which may reflect their confidence in using language generally. For example, a pupil who has a working knowledge of one language already understands the purpose and process of how it works, and is more likely to be able to apply this to another language. The feedback you give to colleagues may be written or verbal depending on the school's policy, but it is best to keep a record of some kind so that the information is available to others if required at a later date.

Brilliant recap

- Always challenge any negative attitudes and stereotyping.
- Encourage and value the contribution of all backgrounds, languages and cultures in school and within the wider community.
- Develop a good relationship with bilingual pupils and their families to encourage home–school communication.
- Make sure you give positive feedback to bilingual pupils when working with them as much as you can.
- Promote multiculturalism and look for diverse resources which may be useful.

Resources

www.equalityhumanrights.com/en – The Equality and Human Rights Commission provides information, guidance and advice for schools around equality.

www.citizensadvice.org.uk has information and support around the Equality Act and schools.

www.equalityadvisoryservice.com – The EASS provide advice and support for those who have experienced discrimination. They also have an equality advisory support service helpline.

www.britishcouncil.org – there is plenty of information here to support the development of relationships with partner schools in other countries.

www.gov.uk – This website has a document entitled Equality Act 2010: advice for schools along with other advice for promoting equality and diversity in 'Related content'.

www.naldic.org.uk – the National Association for English as an Additional Language aims to raise attainment of EAL learners; the website contains a number of links and resources.

Chapter 8

Health, safety and first aid

This chapter will examine the importance of being aware of health and safety issues in your school, as all school staff have a responsibility to maintain the learning environment safely. They should also know the expectations of their role in relation to assisting with the safety and protection of children and young people as well as other adults. This extends to knowing about the Health and Safety at Work Act, risk assessments, following school policy and using safety equipment when needed. You should also know how to respond to sickness, accidents and emergencies and how to record this according to school policy as well as the school's first aid requirements.

Health and safety: Responsibilities and duties for schools

Schools need to ensure that they take measures to protect pupils and adults at all times whilst they are on school premises, and also when accompanying pupils on school trips or walks outside the school. This government document sets out guidelines for health and safety in schools, including roles and responsibilities of staff, risk management and specific control measures. It lists some of the requirements of a school health and safety policy, which should include:

- control measures for health infections
- staff health and safety training
- risk assessment procedures
- recording and reporting accidents
- policies and procedures for off-site visits
- first aid
- health and safety emergencies
- monitoring and reporting the effectiveness of the policy

Control measures for health infections

Pupils will from an early age develop routines and good practice for general personal hygiene and understand its importance. You should be a good role model for pupils, for example talking about the importance of washing your hands after using the toilet, before carrying out cooking activities, or after handling animals. Kitchens and other areas where food is to be prepared should also have their own control measures in place such as the use of gloves.

Staff health and safety training

All schools should offer regular training for staff on health and safety so that they are aware of what to look out for and what to do in different situations. This is especially important for new staff.

Risk assessment procedures

The school is required to carry out risk assessments to determine which areas and activities are most likely to be hazardous, the likelihood of specific hazards occurring and those who are at risk. These should also be recorded although this should not be in detail. Risk assessments should also be carried out when new activities are taking place, for example regarding a venue for a school trip.

Recording and reporting accidents

The school has a duty to record and report any accidents to staff, pupils and visitors.

Policies and procedures for off-site visits

The member of staff responsible will need to fill in specific paperwork which will provide details of transport, distance from school, insurance, adult to pupil ratios and information relevant to the activity which will be undertaken. This will need to be documented so that parents or carers and all of those who are going on the trip are adequately prepared. Parental permission will also need to be gained before taking children off site.

> **Brilliant tip**
>
> When going on residential journeys away from home, always have something up your sleeve to do with pupils – whether this is something art or crafty, word games, or additional audio or films for the coach journey! For primary age pupils, take a special cuddly toy with you for those who are homesick. . . it helps!

First aid

There should be enough first aiders in the school at any time or when on school trips to deal with accidents and first aid, and you should be aware of who they are – schools will usually display their names close to first aid boxes. First aid boxes should be regularly checked and replenished when needed.

Health and safety emergencies such as fire, lockdown and school evacuation procedures

Your school will have procedures in place so that everyone knows what to do in case the building needs to be evacuated or in case of lockdown. Fire drills should take place regularly – at least once a term - and at different times of day. This is to ensure that pupils and all staff are prepared, including midday supervisors and kitchen staff or those responsible for extended school provision.

Monitoring and reporting the effectiveness of the policy

The health and safety policy will need to be regularly monitored and reviewed to ensure that it is still relevant and up to date with current legislation.

Brilliant case study

Errol has been working in a large secondary school for two months and has been working through his induction with his line manager. However, as everyone seems very busy, he has not seen the school health and safety policy and has not had any training on it. He only realises this after the school have a fire drill and he is unsure what to do.

- Should Errol say anything?
- What else could he do in this situation?

General health and safety in the learning environment

As a general rule, you should be vigilant to health and safety issues in all situations, but your routines should help to ensure that you keep the environment free from hazards. Health and safety should be a regular topic at staff meetings, during assemblies and as part of the general school culture so that everyone's attention is drawn to the fact that health and safety is a shared responsibility. Remember also that the younger the child, the less aware of risks they may be in the environment so you will need to modify your level of supervision according to their needs. It will also help younger pupils if you talk to them about why you are doing something safety related, for example, 'I'm just going to move this box because it is blocking a fire exit.'

Ensure rooms are organised and laid out safely

This is common sense but furniture should be the correct size for pupils and well spaced out, and there should always be clear access to fire exits and internal doors. As part of your role as a member of support staff you should assist in keeping equipment organised and in the correct place and encourage pupils to do the same: clear labelling in classrooms and storage areas is a big help. Outdoor areas should also be checked prior to use; for example if you are working in the foundation stage you will routinely need to check for any litter, broken glass or animal mess before children go outside, and sandpits will need to be covered when not in use to ensure that they are clean. If you are working in a specified area of the school grounds, you should also check this before going outside with pupils.

Check furniture, equipment and materials as a matter of course

The person responsible for health and safety in your setting should routinely carry out walkarounds on a regular basis to check that no hazards are left unreported. However, you should also check equipment before using it and if you notice anything broken or damaged, make sure that you remove and label it if possible so that pupils are not able to use it. You should then inform the person responsible – your school may have a book for doing this or you may be able to speak to them directly. All electrical items in school as well as fire equipment should also have annual checks by a qualified person and these should be recorded.

Adapt the environment to ensure safety for any pupils with SEND

All pupils within the class should be given equal opportunities and this should be remembered when setting out the environment. If you are working with a pupil who has special educational needs or disabilities, you will know what considerations or adaptations need to be made for them, particularly if they have larger equipment such as wheelchairs.

Encourage pupils to look out for risk themselves and be a good role model

Pupils should be aware that most activities carry some element of risk. Many children have little opportunity to be independent and to think and explore for themselves, which is an important part of growing up. When carrying out activities, talk to pupils about the kinds of risks you are looking out for so that they start to look for themselves. You should also show that you act safely yourself – pupils will take their lead from you and you should make sure that you do not act in a way which could be dangerous to others. Make sure you show through your own actions that you take safety seriously.

School security and strangers

It is important for schools to know who is on the premises at all times in case of evacuation or lockdown, and to identify anyone who may be acting suspiciously. This means making sure that all those who are in the school have been accounted for through being identified and signed in. Schools will have different ways of doing this, for example visitors may be issued with badges. If you notice any unidentified people in the school, you should challenge them immediately – this can simply be by asking if you can help them in any way. If you notice anything suspicious, you should always send for help. Schools may also have secure entry and exit points, which may make it more difficult for individuals to enter the premises.

Brilliant case study

Gina has just started a job in a new primary school. She is regularly on playground duty and notices that staff often carry cups of tea and coffee outside, particularly in colder weather. They are also able to take hot drinks to their classrooms. Gina is very alert to this as in her previous school there was an accident in which a pupil suffered serious burns after running into an adult who was carrying a hot drink. As she is new she does not wish to appear to be a killjoy; however, she is anxious that the same thing does not happen again.

- Should Gina say anything?
- Can you think of a way in which this could be resolved without upsetting other staff?

Health and Safety at Work etc Act 1974

This act was designed to protect everyone at work through procedures for preventing accidents and the guidelines therefore also apply to school staff. According to the Act, everyone in the workplace is required to observe the procedures below:

Reporting any hazards

All members of the school community should be alert to any hazards in school which might cause injury to themselves or others. Pupils and staff need to be vigilant and immediately report any hazards that they notice to the appropriate person. This may be the school's health and safety representative, or the site manager, headteacher or another member of staff. You should be aware of the designated person to whom you should report health and safety matters and whether this reporting should be written down or verbal.

Following the school's health and safety policy

The school has an obligation to have a health and safety policy which should give information to all staff about the procedures the school has in place to ensure that it is as safe as possible. All new staff joining the school should be given induction training in safety procedures and what to do in case of emergencies. The school should also have a member of staff who is a health and safety representative.

Using any safety equipment and PPE provided

If you carry out any activities with pupils which require you or them to use safety equipment such as tools or goggles, this should always be used. In addition, if you are working with very young children, you may also need to use items like cupboard locks, safety gates, socket covers and window catches. You should always use manufacturers' guidelines when using equipment and it should be checked regularly. There should also be guidelines in the school's policy for the safe use and storage of equipment.

Ensuring that all materials, equipment and resources are safe

Make sure that safety checks are routinely carried out before starting learning activities, particularly when using new equipment. You should always double check that it works before you have pupils with you.

Making sure that your actions do not harm yourselves or others

All staff should ensure that any actions they take are not likely to harm or cause a danger to others in the school. This includes tidying up and putting things away after use. You must also consider the effects of not taking action; for example if you discover a potential hazard – you should not ignore it and it is your responsibility to report it as appropriate.

Controls on substances hazardous to health (COSHH)

The Health and Safety Executive has also set out legal requirements for ensuring that materials in the workplace are stored safely. Anything which could be harmful should be stored out of pupils' reach or locked away in a cupboard – for example, cleaning materials or medicines. COSHH legislation gives a step-by-step list of precautions that need to be taken in order to prevent any risk or injury.

All staff working in a school have a responsibility to ensure that pupils are cared for and safe at all times. The Children Act 1989 and Children (Scotland) Act 1995 also require that staff protect children from risks as far as possible when they are in their care.

E-safety

Most schools will now have an e-safety policy and you will need to know about the associated risks of technology and how to keep pupils safe when online. For more on this, see Chapter 4 on safeguarding.

Brilliant activity

Risk assessments are required to be carried out prior to all school trips, journeys and residential activities. Find out the named person in your school for ensuring that these take place and what kinds of risks need to be documented. What then happens to the paperwork?

Brilliant dos and don'ts

Do

✔ Always be vigilant.

✔ Use and store equipment safely.

✔ Challenge any unidentified people on the premises.

✔ Ensure you know the health and safety procedures in your school.

✔ Carry out risk assessments before doing new activities.

✔ Make sure you know where to find your school's health and safety, first aid and e-safety policies.

Don't

✗ Carry out any activities without being sure that they are safe.

✗ Ignore any hazards – report or remove immediately.

✗ Leave any hazardous materials within the reach of children.

Responding to sickness, accidents and emergencies

Support staff will often be asked to be first aiders in schools and as a result will be on duty at breaks and lunchtimes to tend to playground accidents or any sickness. If you are asked to do this, you will need to be sent on first aid training, which should be renewed every three years. You should not attempt to carry out any first aid or treat a casualty unless you have had the correct training – if you are the only adult in the vicinity, you must make sure that you follow the correct procedures until help arrives. This should be a qualified first aider and, if necessary, an ambulance. You will need to support and reassure not only the casualty but also other pupils who may be present. Others may be distressed depending on what they have witnessed, or may be in shock themselves. Make sure that you and any others on the scene are not put at any unnecessary risk.

Following the incident you will also be required to fill in the school's documentation so that there is a record of the accident and of any treatment which has been carried out. This is a legal requirement under RIDDOR (Reporting of Injuries, Diseases and Dangerous Occurrences Regulations 2013). In some schools, particularly with younger pupils, you may need to phone parents or carers, or send home a brief note stating treatment which has been given. It is particularly important to tell parents or carers if their child has had a bump on the head in case they suffer from any concussion. Accident forms will also need to be completed for any adults who are involved in accidents at work so that these are correctly documented.

Deer Lane Primary School Accident Report Form

Name of casualty ....

Exact location of incident ....

Date and time ....

What was the injured person doing? ....

How did the accident happen? ....

What injuries were sustained? ....

Treatment given ....

Medical aid sought? ....

Name of person dealing with incident ....

Name of witness ....

If the casualty was a child, at what time were parents/carers informed?

....

Was hospital attended? ....

Was the accident investigated? ....

Signed ....

Brilliant tip

When recording and reporting accidents, do this as soon as possible after the event so that you can remember all of the details.

Dealing with common illnesses

As you get to know the pupils with whom you work, it is likely that you will be able to identify times when they are not 'themselves' or are unwell. Remember that depending on their age or their needs, some pupils may not be able to communicate exactly what is wrong. General signs that children are 'off colour' could include:

- temperature
- pale skin
- flushed cheeks
- rashes
- different (quiet, clingy, irritable) behaviour
- rings around the eyes

- sore throat
- loss of appetite
- general fatigue

Some of these symptoms are common to different illnesses and infections, so if you have any concerns about a pupil always discuss them with another member of staff. Children will often develop symptoms more quickly than adults, as they may have less resistance to infection, so it may be important to act quickly. Most schools will call parents or carers straightaway if their child is showing signs or symptoms of illness. The Department of Health has also issued a useful poster, 'Guidance on infection control in schools and nurseries', which could be displayed in the first aid area as a quick reference as it sets out some common illnesses and their characteristics. You are also likely to find that head lice and viruses such as coughs and colds and chickenpox are quite commonplace in schools as it is easy for infections to spread quickly in such a close environment.

Symptoms which mean that the pupil requires immediate medical attention may be:

- raised temperature (along with other symptoms such as a rash)
- rash (along with other symptoms such as a temperature, a stiff neck/headache)
- unresponsive
- problems breathing

In each of these situations, the symptoms may be caused by an allergic reaction or an existing medical condition, or may also be signs of bacterial meningitis. You should contact your first aider and call 999 or 112 immediately.

Pupils' general wellbeing

As well as looking for signs of illness, you should be on the lookout for any pupils who may be struggling with their mental health and wellbeing. Any of the following could be indicators that a pupil needs support:

- poor appearance
- lack of appetite
- negative self-concept
- self-harming or bulimia
- changes in/inappropriate behaviour
- regularly missing school

In these situations you should raise your concerns with teachers or the Designated Safeguarding Lead (DSL) in the first instance in case there has already been some support put in place which you do not know about. However, it is important that you do not ignore it. (For more on safeguarding and pastoral care, see Chapter 4.)

Brilliant case study

Carey is concerned about one of the Year 6 pupils she does a maths intervention with each day. He has recently become very withdrawn and has missed quite a bit of school. She has asked him if he is okay a couple of times but he has just shrugged and said yes. He has also expressed some anxiety about transferring to secondary school.

- Write a short list of the steps that Carey could take in this situation.

Emergencies

An emergency is any situation which can endanger life. Some examples of these in school may be:

- fires, gas leaks or bomb scares
- serious burns

- loss of consciousness
- choking
- a missing child or young person

Your school will have procedures for dealing with emergencies and you will need to know about these so that you are ready for any emergency situations.

Brilliant activity

Make sure you know your school's policy for emergencies and the identity of first aiders so that you are well prepared. Also check the location of any documentation so that you know where it is kept.

Allergies and allergic reactions

In most schools there will be a number of pupils who have allergic reactions or intolerances to foods such as nuts, wheat or citrus fruits. All school staff should be aware of the identities of those pupils who have allergies, and clear instructions on how to deal with each case should be readily available. In particular, those on duty at lunchtimes or in extended school provision need to be kept informed, particularly if there are any changes or if new pupils arrive in school who have allergies. Staff should also be provided with training if they are asked to treat pupils who have allergies with EpiPens (EpiPens are used to treat extreme allergic reactions and anaphylactic shock). There may be a book or information folder for staff containing photos of relevant pupils, information about their allergies and contact telephone numbers. In some schools, photos and information may be displayed on staff room walls. However, care must always be taken to keep pupil information confidential.

Medicines and medical conditions

As well as allergies, there will be pupils in school who have medical conditions such as asthma, epilepsy or others which require medication to be administered. Any medication which is in school will usually be kept in the school office and again this should be documented so that it can be checked if necessary. Sometimes asthma pumps or EpiPens may also be kept in classrooms in case they are needed urgently, and they should be labelled and updated regularly so that they are up to date.

Brilliant tip

Make sure you are aware of pupils that you work with who have allergies and medical conditions. Your SENDCo or school office may be a good place to start.

Brilliant recap

- Be vigilant at all times for any dangers to others' safety and security.
- Check the environment as well as equipment and resources as a matter of course.
- Be aware of your school's health and safety policy.
- Make sure you have had any training if you are asked to administer first aid.

References

www.bbc.co.uk/health/firstaid – Guide to First Aid

www.hse.gov.uk – Health and Safety Executive

www.gov.uk – Health and safety responsibilities and duties for schools 2021

www.gov.uk – Health and safety on educational visits 2018

Chapter 9

Extended school provision

The extended schools programme was launched in 2003 and was introduced to develop the kinds of facilities which are on offer to pupils and their families in both primary and secondary schools. Although the funding for the programme was withdrawn in 2011, many schools continue to operate extended schools provision as much as possible as it has been proven to have positive benefits to children and families and to reduce inequality, although there are inconsistencies in what is available (Carpenter et al., 2011). Most schools still offer a range of activities and support services for pupils and families along with breakfast and after-school clubs. They may also offer wraparound care which includes school holiday provision as well as childcare, and a variety of enrichment activities which benefit children's holistic development as well as benefitting families and the wider community.

More and more, teaching assistants are supporting and leading sessions during out-of-school clubs, extended hours provision, holiday clubs and other activities which may take place inside or outside school hours. Although it should not be a requirement of your role, the kinds of opportunities which running these activities provide could be good for your own personal and professional development and raise your profile both within the school and also the wider community. In this chapter, we will look at some different examples of how you might support pupils as well as other staff in this wider context and how to manage different activities and situations.

Breakfast and after-school clubs

Breakfast and after-school clubs are now part of the day in many primary schools.

As part of the Extended Schools programme, breakfast and after-school clubs became known as 'wraparound childcare' in some authorities and enabled parents and carers of primary school aged children to leave them on site from early in the morning before the start of school until early in the evening, depending on their requirements. They are also able to select the days and times which are best for them although the provision may have waiting lists. For children, they provide a safe place as well as a nutritious breakfast or after-school snack, as in some cases children may not have access to this at home.

The development of breakfast and after-school clubs has meant that many school sites are open for longer and will also offer other clubs to pupils if they have the staff or facilities. Breakfast and after-school clubs may be run by an external organisation or individual on the school site although they may also be run by or employ existing support staff. Breakfast and after-school clubs are also required to be registered and fulfil Ofsted criteria as well as being liable for inspection, although this will take place separately under the education inspection framework. If they are responsible for Reception-age children, they will also need to meet the statutory requirements of the early years foundation stage. It is likely that they will provide meals and snacks for pupils and also run a range of activities within the space and time available.

If you are part of breakfast or after-school provision your role will follow the principles of playwork (a profession which sets out to enrich children's play without the need to be driven by education or care requirements) and will be different from that which you have during the day, and you are likely to be working with groups of children and carrying out creative or recreational activities with them rather than supporting teaching and learning. However, in some schools there may also be additional support with homework during these times if there is a quiet area that the children can use as well as staff availability.

If you are responsible for preparing food such as breakfast, you will need to ensure that you meet the basic requirements for food hygiene. Those preparing and handling food should have a Level 2 Food Safety and Hygiene certificate.

Brilliant example

Rhianna works at a large primary school. During the day she works in years 5 and 6 but before school starts she works in the breakfast club which provides childcare for pupils whose parents need this additional facility. Rhianna runs some play and creative activities for the children and also gives them breakfast alongside the breakfast club co-ordinator. Sometimes children in the club will have school duties such as taking round the registers before the start of school and Rhianna ensures that everyone has a chance to do this regularly.

Extra-curricular activities

As you get to know the school and other staff, you may find that some of them run extra-curricular activities for children. These may be before or after school, or sometimes during lunchtimes, and so are different from breakfast and after-school provision which is more childcare based. Schools may plan these extra-curricular activities according to need or requests by the pupils. They may also offer clubs based on the particular strengths of some members of staff; for example a member of staff who is ex-military may run outward bound or forest school sessions, or someone who is good at crafting may offer to run a craft club. In some schools, all staff are required to support extra-curricular activities in some way, whilst in others it is based on whether or not staff wish to run them.

If you are providing extra-curricular activities, you may be supporting or leading extended hours provision in the form of clubs or organised sessions which pupils attend in your school on a daily or weekly basis. Depending on your responsibilities you may be asked to plan activities yourself for pupils or to work with others to do this. The kinds of activities which take place as part of extended school provision will vary from school to school and depend on the age and needs of pupils. They may include the following:

- play and recreational activities
- fitness classes
- drama
- sport
- musical activities
- study support
- arts, crafts and other special interest clubs
- volunteering and business and enterprise activities
- Duke of Edinburgh Award scheme

If you are interested in running a club or extra- curricular activity, you should speak to your line manager who will be able to look with you at what the school is running already and whether there are facilities to run the club. For example, if the hall is already booked for another club on a specific day it may not be possible.

Brilliant examples

Tom works in a secondary school as a learning support assistant for a pupil in Year 9. He has an interest in basketball and is a qualified coach, and has just started to run a basketball club on Mondays after school for pupils in Years 7 and 8.

Migena works in Year 2 with a teacher who is the school's music co-ordinator. As she is a competent pianist she has asked the teacher whether she can develop her skills and extend herself professionally by getting more involved with music in the school. She has accompanied the key stage 1 and 2 choirs on several occasions and helps with the rehearsals during lunchtime once a week.

These kinds of extra activities will give pupils the opportunity to try out tasks and activities which they may not otherwise have the chance to, and also encourage them to try new things and extend their skills and knowledge. You may find that some pupils in your school are enthusiastic about trying as many as they can, whilst others may not join any. There may also be some activities which are more popular than others and the school may need to review the kinds of activities which are on offer depending on the resources available.

Although you may be supporting a teacher or another colleague in delivering extra-curricular activities, if you are in sole charge you will have a number of additional responsibilities and will need to bear these in mind.

Health and safety

Observing health and safety law is a requirement of which you will need to be fully aware. As well as knowing your school's health and safety policy (see Chapter 8), you will also have additional responsibility during the session for ensuring that pupils are aware of what to do in case they need to evacuate the building, making sure that they behave safely at all times and encouraging them to think about safety when carrying out activities. You will also need to know about any health needs of the pupils (e.g. asthma or any allergies) in case they need access to medication whilst they are in your care.

Safe removal, use and storage of equipment

Make sure before you start to run your activity that you have checked any equipment which is required and are able to access it at the time it is needed. You may need to take it through another room which is being used by others or have to remove it from locked cupboards or storage rooms. Make sure you have enough for the number of pupils who will be attending and that if they need to, they bring appropriate kit or additional items – if necessary write a letter to parents and carers outlining what will be required. Following the activity, you will need to replace any school equipment and make sure that it is stored safely and securely.

Making sure you set clear ground rules for behaviour

You will need to make a point of doing this so that the group are clear on what they are expected to do and know the rules of the activity. This is especially important if you are using tools or equipment but you should do it in every instance so that pupils are clear from the outset (see also Chapter 5).

Keeping registers or logs of attendance

You should always ensure that you comply with the school's regulations for checking attendance. You should have been provided with a list or register of names so that you know who is present and can sign pupils in at the start and out at the end. Even if you think that you know exactly who has arrived, it is very easy for one person to be missed, and you will be accountable for each pupil who is present. You will also need to be very clear about collection arrangements and who has left at the end of the activity.

Brilliant dos and don'ts – Running an extra-curricular activity

Do

✔ Before you start the club, find out whether the activity is something that the pupils will be interested in doing.

✔ Take time to plan and think about the format.

✔ Emphasise the importance of good behaviour and timekeeping.

✔ Make sure you give pupils the opportunity to evaluate the activity and give their own suggestions.

Don't

✗ Put yourself forward unless you are able to be there every week – it is important not to let pupils down.

✗ Compromise on safety.

✗ Forget to check any tools or equipment regularly.

Brilliant tip

If you are thinking of offering to run a club or activity because you have an interest or would like to extend your experience, go and observe and support a colleague in your school first and make a note of the kinds of things which they need to do in addition to organising the pupils and their activities.

Brilliant case study

Saskia is an experienced support assistant and in addition has just started to run a small craft club for key stage 2 after school. She has the use of a classroom and has a group of twelve children for the activities. Saskia has taken a register of pupils at the beginning so knows who is present but following the club, one of the Year 6 children tells her that she is allowed to walk home on her own. Ten minutes later her mother comes to collect her and although she is late, tells Saskia that she did not give her permission to walk home on her own and that she will be speaking to the headteacher straightaway.

- How should Saskia have responded to the girl's request?
- What should she do now to support the parent?

Further extended school provision

When extended schools were launched, families were involved in discussions about the kinds of services which would benefit the community. Subsequently, schools and local authorities introduced a range of provision catering for different needs and requirements. These were based in different schools in the area according to the requirements of the community and the facilities available in each; for example some schools have their own swimming pools or others their own athletics track. In primary schools extended services have tended to focus around childcare and additional extra-curricular activities although additional services such as parenting support and other courses may also be available through outside organisations. In secondary schools, the aim has been to develop provision so that they will offer both curriculum-based and additional courses such as first aid or computing courses for pupils and the wider community. They may also work with young people on community projects and voluntary work, and in some cases work with local primary schools through activities such as reading support. Working with local authorities, many schools will now also provide facilities or additional services for pupils in other schools and for the wider community through working in cluster groups to deliver co-ordinated provision. The kinds of organisations which may be involved within the community are as follows.

Adult education services

Adult education may be able to offer classes and additional training to young people and to parents and carers. In some cases creative, English language or educational classes are offered for parents alongside their children. This can also have benefits for those parents or carers who may see schools as threatening or who have had bad experiences themselves in order to encourage them to have more confidence to have contact with schools.

Brilliant example

Callie runs an art group for children and their parents as part of the extended schools programme. As well as working as a learning support assistant three days per week, she is an art teacher for the local adult education group. She has been able to work with her school to set up and run the group using some of the school's resources and this has encouraged many parents and carers to become more involved with the school as well as developing good relationships and learning alongside their children.

Health and social care services

The range of services which are required at some stage by children and young people are diverse. They may include the input of professionals such as speech and language therapists, behavioural support services, or occupational and physiotherapists. In some cases, special schools in communities may be able to offer wider access to these kinds of services for all pupils through creating more streamlined support services.

All schools are being encouraged to work towards achieving healthy schools status, which requires them to meet a number of criteria in areas such as physical activity, healthy eating and emotional well being and this should also be supported by the extended schools programme.

Children's centres

In some areas, remaining children's centres offer wider services including health and family support and referral. In some cases children's centres are being linked directly to schools, which is more straightforward for both children and parents and carers as this will mean that pupils' childcare and school experience will be on one site. However, many children's centres have unfortunately been forced to close in recent years, which means that some of these services are more difficult to access for parents and carers.

Although these additional services are mainly based in schools, the expectation is that they will not be run by existing teachers. Support staff, volunteers and professionals within the wider community should all be involved in providing the kinds of services which are needed and you may have the opportunity to contribute in some way if this is something that interests you. In this case you should speak to your line manager to register an interest. Parents and carers should also be involved at every level in making sure that the kinds of services which are on offer are a reflection of what is needed within the community. It is important for the success of the programme that parents or carers are encouraged to contribute ideas and become involved in the development of extended schools as much as possible.

Brilliant activity

Find out about the kind of extended school provision which is available both through your own school and in your local academy group or family of schools. If necessary, you may be able to find out through your local authority about what is available.

Brilliant case study

Rob runs the local scout group and the venue he has been using has just told him that they will be unable to carry on using it due to building work over the next few months. As he also works at the local secondary school as a member of support staff, he has had the idea of booking the school hall and also offering Duke of Edinburgh award training to pupils from the surrounding area as an extra activity.

- Would Rob be able to do this?
- Where might he go for support in order to see his idea through?

Taking pupils on school trips

It is important for all pupils to have the opportunity to explore different environments both through the provision of outdoor learning environments and through having access to school trips and journeys. Support staff will regularly be asked to assist on school trips, in particular if they have an additional skill such as being a first aider. If you support an individual pupil it will also be part of your role to go with them and support them. Depending on the age of pupils and the purpose of the trip, it may also involve taking part in additional activities. You will need to be particularly aware of safety when taking pupils out of school; if you are taking a large number of pupils on an outing or residential trip, the trip organiser should carry out a risk assessment beforehand. This means that they will check what kinds of risks there might be during the trip and the likelihood of it occurring. The level of risk may depend on a number of factors:

- the adult/pupil ratio
- where you are going
- the activities the pupils will be undertaking
- transport to the venue and back

Risk assessment comprises of assessing the level of risk in each instance and then filling in a form to show what action will be taken to avoid this from occurring.

The facilities will need to be checked to make sure that they are adequate for the needs of the pupils, for example if you are taking a large number of children or young people, or a pupil who has a disability. As well as a risk assessment, preparations need to include other considerations. A trip will always be planned thoroughly so that the adults are prepared for whatever happens. Preparations include the need to:

- seek and gain parental consent
- arrange for suitable safe transport (with plenty of notice! Coach companies get booked up long in advance)
- take a first aid kit and first aider as well as inhalers or medication for pupils who may need them
- take appropriate clothing for the activity or weather
- make lists of adults and the pupils for whom they will be responsible
- give information sheets to all helpers, including timings and any safety information
- make sure pupils you may have concerns about are in your group rather than with a volunteer helper

Brilliant tip

Ask the teacher who is organising a school trip to talk you through what is required in advance so that you are fully prepared. Never leave reading it through until the last minute.

As a member of support staff you will not be responsible for making all of these checks but it is helpful to be aware of them so that you can ask the teacher who is organising the trip if anything is not clear.

Brilliant dos and don'ts – Going on school trips

Do

✔ Make sure you are thoroughly prepared before the day and have everything ready.

✔ Check that you are aware of the health needs of pupils in your group and have any medication with you.

✔ Offer support to any parents and carers or volunteers who may not have been on a trip before.

✔ Remember any time constraints when you are out.

Don't

✗ Take anything into your own hands without informing the trip co-ordinator.

✗ Relax – you are in a position of responsibility at all times!

✗ Forget – the younger the children, the less they will be aware of safety issues.

Brilliant recap

- Breakfast and after-school club hours will vary according to the needs of the community.
- Extended school provision may take the form of additional clubs and extra-curricular activities as well as breakfast and after-school clubs.
- You should not have to carry out extended school duties as part of your role but it may be a valuable form of professional development.

References

H. Carpenter et al. (2011) Extended Services in Practice: a summary of evaluation evidence for headteachers, Department for Education.

Further information

https://cpag.org.uk/policy-and-campaigns/extended-schools: The Child Poverty Action Group gives further information about extended school provision.

https://www.outofschoolalliance.co.uk/about-out-of-school-clubs: Information on out of school clubs.

Chapter 10

Reflecting on your practice and continuing professional development

The role of the teaching assistant has changed dramatically in recent years. In 2022, there were 281,000 teaching assistants in schools, an increase of 91,000 since 2010. It has been professionalised as the number of support staff has risen and there is now a huge range of roles and responsibilities within schools which come under this job title. This chapter will look at the importance of reflecting on your own practice and considering your continuing professional development through the appraisal process, also known as continuing professional development. It will include looking at how you can keep up to date with career developments as well as national and local requirements. This will also put you in a stronger position when applying for different jobs within the education sector. It is important to know how to approach looking for new jobs, writing your CV and going to interviews. Finally, you should think about different ways in which you can manage work/life balance, particularly if you have a family of your own.

Continuing professional development and the appraisal process

Teaching assistants are increasingly part of the whole school staff appraisal process. This means that in the same way that teachers need to review their performance each year and look at targets to work towards, support staff will be asked to meet with their line manager to do the same thing. This should not be seen as worrying or threatening and is designed to support you in thinking about what you do and how you carry out reflective practice (see Figure 10.1).

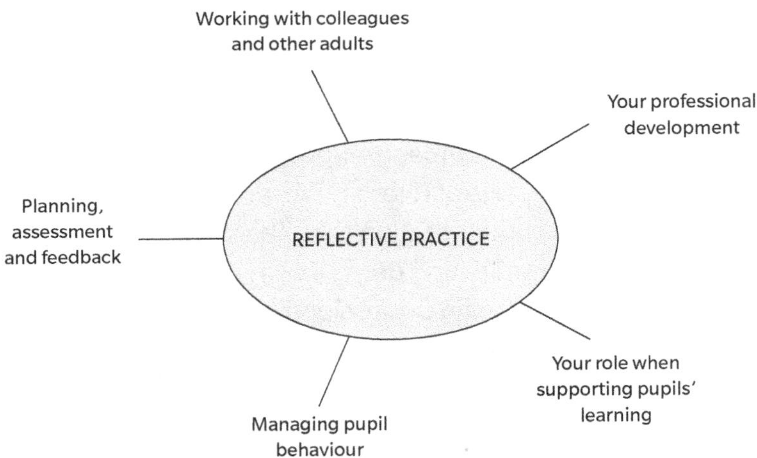

Figure 10.1 Your reflective practice

Reflective practice is the process of looking at your own professional actions in different areas and thinking about ways in which you might set goals in order to change or improve your practice. As part of the appraisal process, it is an opportunity to discuss and evaluate your role and to consider the kinds of changes that could be made. It relates not only to your professional development but also to how you carry out individual activities with pupils and to other aspects of your role. You need to reflect on a regular basis and should have the opportunity to discuss your thoughts and your ideas with your colleagues; in this way you will be able to identify areas of strength as well as exploring those which may need further development. Support staff will often have quite diverse roles in schools and inevitably you will find that you are more confident in some areas than in others; by reflecting on your practice and how you work with your colleagues you will become more effective in your role and gain confidence.

Brilliant example

Tamsin has been working within the same year group (Y1) for several years. She enjoys her work and gets on well with the class teacher and feels quite confident in her work. The school has just introduced performance management for teaching assistants and as part of this process, she reflects on her knowledge and skills and as a consequence, goes on a training course to update her computer skills. Although she had not considered this before her appraisal, following the course she is much more confident and is able to use technology more in her practice with pupils.

When carrying out reflective practice as part of the appraisal process, you should have the opportunity to consider different aspects of your role prior to any meeting with your line manager. You may wish to use the headings in Figure 10.1 in order to help you to gather ideas. In this way you will be more prepared for the meeting and able to put your suggestions forward.

Your professional development

As you are employed as a professional, you should be able to think about your role on a regular basis. This means looking at your own job description and thinking about different areas of development. It might be helpful to consider different ways in which you can extend your knowledge and try new things.

Your role when supporting pupils' learning

You should take some time to look at different activities which you have carried out with individuals or groups of pupils and evaluate how the sessions went. However experienced you are, you should always consider different ways of approaching teaching and learning activities. It may also be helpful for your line manager or another colleague to observe you working with pupils as part of your appraisal so that they can also help you to evaluate your practice.

Brilliant tip

If you are new to your role or have taken on a different year group or subject it may be beneficial to you to ask teachers for some general feedback about your work with pupils. This may be useful if you do not have appraisal in your school or if this will not take place for some time.

Managing pupil behaviour

This can be one of the more challenging aspects of your work. You will need to work as part of a whole school approach to behaviour management, which should set out the kinds of strategies you are able to use with pupils. In order to manage behaviour effectively you will need to be consistent with pupils so that they understand boundaries and are aware of why we need to have them. Some pupils may also need support with social and emotional issues and with their mental health, and you may need additional training if you are working with these pupils. By reflecting on how you manage behaviour and how this relates to whole school practice, you will start to consider how to do this effectively. (For more on behaviour management, see Chapter 5.)

Planning, assessment and feedback

You may or may not be involved in the planning process, but it is important that you know what has been planned in the classes you support and what it involves for you. This is so that you can prepare for the lessons and consider your approach. It is also important that you have some opportunity to give feedback to teachers following learning activities; as your role is supporting teaching and learning, your feedback will inform the next cycle of planning. Make sure you know:

- the learning objectives for each session
- whether any of the pupils have special educational needs or have particular targets to work on
- pupils' backgrounds and circumstances which may affect their behaviour or learning
- How you will feed back to the teacher (is this written or verbal, at a set time or planned?)

As part of your performance management, reflect on how much you are involved in different aspects of planning, assessment and feedback, and whether this could be improved.

Working with colleagues and other adults

Your relationships with your colleagues are important as communication is a key part of your work with pupils. Think about how you relate to others in your school and the support you offer them within various teams you may belong to (year group, subject area, class, key stage). If you support a pupil who has special educational needs, you may also work with teams of professionals who are external to the school, such as educational psychologists or speech therapists. It is also likely that you will work with parents and carers, particularly if you work closely with one pupil. When considering this aspect of your role you should think about the ways in which you can develop your relationships with others so that pupils are supported more effectively.

Brilliant dos and don'ts

Do

- ✔ Be honest with yourself and others.
- ✔ Think about all aspects of your work.
- ✔ Include both successes and failures.
- ✔ Ask a colleague for help if you need it.

Don't

- ✗ Worry about your appraisal – it is meant to help you in your role.
- ✗ Forget that all members of staff including the headteacher will go through the same process.
- ✗ Try to develop everything at once – your targets will need to be achievable.

Following this preparation, you will set a date for your initial appraisal meeting with your line manager or the member of staff who is responsible for teaching assistants in the school. This may for example be the deputy headteacher or the SENDCo if you are an individual support assistant. The structure of the meeting will depend on your own school's approach but it is likely that you will consider your job description in the light of what you do on a day-to-day basis and think about whether it is still a reflection of your role. You may then talk through your classroom observation if you have had one, and think about any issues which have come up as a result of this. Finally, you might discuss the aspects of your job which give you the most and least satisfaction and think about any additional training which you would find helpful following your reflection on your role. You will then think about three or four targets to work on over the next twelve months. These targets may comprise of any training which you will be doing anyway, such as attending a safeguarding course as part of the school staff or completing a teaching assistant qualification. They may also include working on aspects of your role which have special interest for you, such as supporting pupils with dyslexia or other specific learning needs.

Brilliant tip

Make sure your targets are SMART:

- Specific: Ensure your target says exactly what is required.
- Measurable: Make sure you can measure whether the target has been achieved.
- Achievable: The target should not be inaccessible or too difficult.
- Realistic: Ensure you have access to the training or resources that may be required.
- Time-bound: There should be a limit to the time you have available to achieve your target. This is because otherwise you may continually put it off to another date!

The main points of your conversation will then be documented by your line manager and then the targets recorded in a format such as the one below.

Professional Review Meeting

Name .... Date ....

Line manager ....

Areas discussed ....

Review of last year's targets (if applicable)

New targets for professional development:

1)

2)

3)

To be reviewed on:

Signed .... (TA)

.... (Line manager)

Keeping up to date with career developments

You will usually be able to keep up with the kinds of courses and development opportunities which are available to support staff through your school. You may find that the school invites people from different outside agencies to speak to or train staff during staff meetings or INSET days and these may be optional or obligatory for support staff. Your line manager or supervisor should be able to give you advice and information about training and help you to decide on the best courses or meetings to attend. Additionally your SENDCo may be able to give you details of any courses to support your work with pupils who have special educational needs. If you have any difficulty finding help, your local education authority will publish details of courses well in advance. You should also keep up to date through reading educational publications or websites such as the TES, or joining online social media groups specifically for teaching assistants, for example Twinkl and Facebook groups.

Brilliant case study

Jack is working as an individual support assistant for a blind pupil in a secondary school. He has been there for two years and although he is very experienced and well trained for his work with the pupil he does not have any qualifications but he has been investigating some of his options. He would like to be better qualified as there is a possibility that his pupil may be moving schools; however, he does not have much contact with his line manager as he is not full time and there are no points of contact during the week.

- What should Jack do first?
- Is there anything else he could do if the school did not support his request?

Over the past 20 years there have been many developments in the qualifications and courses available for support staff. Although it is not a requirement to have a formal qualification for this role, teaching assistants may be qualified at level 1, 2 or 3, or have been awarded Higher Level Teaching Assistant (HLTA) status, although this is not a qualification. In addition, a number of courses are available for those who support children and young people who have different special educational needs.

There is also some confusion about different levels and whether there should be a pay scale for support staff as pay and conditions vary between local authorities. Local authorities in different areas may give teaching assistants job titles which reflect their level of experience or expertise. For example, in some LA's, support staff who deal mainly with administrative tasks such as displays and so on may be called classroom assistants, whereas those who are more involved with supporting teaching and learning are teaching assistants; this is not however a national requirement.

It is important when looking at qualifications to have good advice and to choose the right one for you because many of them are work based so will give a good indication of the level at which you are working. Although there is no formal requirement for teaching assistants to have a qualification, those who undertake them will say that they enhance and improve their practice and will add to their CV when applying for jobs. If you can, ask others about courses that they have been on so that you can find out which most appeal or may be useful to you. Courses may be full or part time and depending on your hours at school you may have to speak to your headteacher for time out in order to study. Alternatively, some centres offer evening courses so that you can attend outside school hours.

Brilliant tip

From the start of your career, always keep a record of all courses you attend and qualifications gained. They will be a good record of your professional development and will be useful for you to have to hand if you need to update your CV or attend an interview.

Making a job application

Whatever your role, it is likely that at some stage you will need to think about changing your job. It can be fairly daunting to do this, particularly if you have been in the same school for some time.

In many cases, teaching assistants have started their careers by volunteering in their own child's school and gradually building up their role and experience and may feel disloyal or lack confidence in looking elsewhere. However, you may have more experience than you think and if you have been on additional training or have developed areas of speciality you may find that it is appealing to consider working in another school or even changing key stages. Before you even apply to a different school, find out as much about it as you can and visit it if possible. You should make sure that you check the advertisement or person specification to ensure that you have the required experience or qualifications if necessary. It is likely that you will need to give the names of references – one of these should always be your current headteacher so it is very important to check with them first.

Brilliant tip

Having an up-to-date CV which you revise every year or so can be a useful additional document to have to hand if needed when considering a new role.

Writing a CV or filling in an application form?

When making an application, you will find that some advertisements will ask you to fill in an online form, whereas others may ask you to send your CV with a covering letter. You will need to make sure that you do this carefully – never write it straight out without making a draft first in case you need to change it. Your supporting statement or covering letter will need to be well written and show how you fulfil the requirements of the person specification. You should use it to sell yourself and to say why you are the best person for the post, so include details such as relevant previous experience, additional training you may have attended, or specific areas of expertise.

If you are writing a CV you should always include a number of essential details:

- name
- address
- other contact details (email, phone numbers)
- date of birth (this is no longer a legal requirement, so not necessary if you prefer not to)
- qualifications
- employment history (start with your most recent employer and make sure any gaps in employment are explained, for example having children, travel etc.)
- other interests and relevant experiences, for example running a scout group or Duke of Edinburgh award, first aider, sports coach, guitar player etc.

> **Brilliant tip**
>
> Always ask another person to check your application and supporting statement for you before sending them.

Going to interviews

Going to an interview will always be a useful experience and you should try to view it as such, even if you are nervous. Remember that as well as the school finding out if you would be the right person for the post, you are also finding out about whether the school is right for you. Try to give yourself plenty of time to arrive and dress comfortably without being too casual or overly confident. Remember that first impressions will be part of the process!

There are some key questions which you may be asked – try to be prepared by having some answers ready in advance. You may also be able to ask other assistants in your school for the kinds of questions they have been asked at interviews.

Brilliant example

- Why have you applied for this role?
- What kind of experience have you had?
- What have been your most/least satisfying experiences in the classroom?
- What would you do if a parent approached you with a question about their child's progress?
- What should you do if you have concerns around safeguarding?
- Outline different examples of how you might promote a pupil's independence in the classroom.
- How should you approach the management of pupil behaviour?

Brilliant dos and don'ts

Do

✔ Think about the interview beforehand and be prepared for some of the more common questions.

✔ Make eye contact with those who are interviewing you.

✔ Try to relax during the interview.

✔ Listen to each question carefully so that you are clear on what is being asked.

✔ Have one or two questions ready to ask afterwards.

✔ Smile and make sure you thank the panel at the end.

Don't

✗ Wear clothes which make you stand out for the wrong reasons (e.g. t-shirts with slogans, short skirt, loud suit, comedy tie, plunging neckline).

- ✗ Panic – the panel may be just as nervous as you!
- ✗ Try to answer questions straightaway if you need to think for a moment.
- ✗ Be dishonest. If you haven't had the experience or don't know the answer, say so.

Maintaining a work/life balance

One of the more challenging aspects of your role can be maintaining a work/life balance. You may have started part time and been asked to increase your hours, or have just returned to work after having a family. There will always be times when it can seem difficult to juggle your different roles; this can be exacerbated if you decide to go on additional training, particularly if this takes place over several months. It can sometimes seem as though everything happens at once, for example if you have started a new job while one of your own children has just started secondary school. However, many teaching assistants and other support staff are in a similar position, often as single parents or with other additional pressures, and there are some ways in which you can plan and use your time more effectively.

Plan to have some you time each week

You should make sure that even if this is just for a couple of hours, you have some time away from being mum/dad/TA/student so that you have something to look forward to, whether this is a hobby or socialising with friends.

Plan your time carefully

You may need to review how you use your time – this may mean sorting out meals a week in advance, having your groceries delivered, or allocating housework to specific days of the week. People with less time often seem to manage to do more through careful time management.

Make the most of any offers of help or arrange some swaps with friends

If you have friends with children of a similar age, arrange some childcare swaps so that you get more time to yourself if possible.

Speak to your own family and enlist their help

Even if each person has one responsibility each week this will mean that you have less to do.

Join any TA forums or networks

This may help you with any study you are doing and can also help you to feel that you are not alone.

Whilst there will always be times in which you may feel that there are not enough hours in the day, your work with pupils should give you plenty of job satisfaction and be very rewarding. There are also many more opportunities for you now as the role of the teaching assistant develops to extend your skills and expertise and you may decide to take your career in a different direction through your experiences.

Brilliant recap

- Prepare carefully for your appraisal through careful reflection.
- Try to keep up to date by reading educational publications and looking online.
- Keep finding ways to extend yourself as part of your role.
- Make sure your CV and record of professional development is up to date.
- Prepare carefully for interviews.
- Try to actively maintain a good work/life balance.

Further reading

www.tes.co.uk – The Times Educational Supplement.

www.napta.org.uk – National Association of Professional Teaching Assistants.

www.twinkl.co.uk – This website has a section for teaching assistants including resources, training and additional information.

www.open.edu/openlearn/education-development/resources-teaching-assistants – Information and support for career progression.

www.maximisingtas.co.uk – Research, articles and information from the MITA programme.

Twitter groups.

Facebook groups.

The Little Book of Reflective Practice (early years based): Annie Pendrey (David Fulton, 2022).

Unions for TAs

Unison – www.unison.org.uk

GMB – www.gmb.org.uk

Unite – www.unitetheunion.org/

Appendix 1: Case study solutions

Chapter 1

Brilliant case study

Emma has just spent break talking to Lorraine, who is another teaching assistant working in key stage 3. She has found some challenges in her work with a particular pupil that Lorraine supported the previous year. Lorraine is able to talk through some of the strategies which worked and which she may find useful.

- In what ways will this chat be useful?
- How else might Lorraine be able to help Emma long term?

Solution

This chat will be useful as another teaching assistant will be fully aware of the kinds of challenges which Emma is facing. As well as having more time than teachers, Lorraine will be able to understand how to deal with the pupil from the same point of view and it will be more helpful for Emma to hear her talking about what she found worked best. She may also be able to help by discussing how she worked with teachers when supporting the pupil and whether any outside agencies have been involved or given advice.

Brilliant case study

Sina works in a small village primary school as a teaching assistant in Year 2. Her child is in another class and her best friend is also a parent at the school. Sina's friend regularly tries to find out what happens in the class on a daily basis and often questions her on the way home about specific children. She is also very keen that her child is put up to the next level in reading and asks Sina to 'sort it out' for her.

- What should Sina do in this situation?
- Why is it important that she does not talk to her friend about what happens in class?

Solution

It is very important that Sina explains to her friend that she has a responsibility for confidentiality as part of her role within the school and that it is not appropriate to discuss other children with her. She is taking advantage of her relationship with Sina but also putting her in a very difficult position and jeopardising her job. Playgrounds are often the place where rumours and gossip start and Sina should not be made a part of this. In addition, if Sina's friend is not happy with her child's progress it should be pointed out to her that she should make an appointment with the class teacher. If her friend persists, Sina should seek advice and further support from her line manager.

Chapter 2

Brilliant case study

Myra is working in a small one form entry primary school and usually floats between Years 1 and 2. The teaching assistant who has worked in the Reception class for the last few years has gone on maternity leave and as cover is needed, Myra has been asked to step in for a few months. She does not have experience of the EYFS and soon starts to feel that she needs more support.

- Where should Myra go for support in the first instance?
- Is there anywhere else Myra could seek help?

Solution

Myra should go either to her line manager or to the foundation stage manager and talk through her concerns as soon as possible, particularly if she is anxious about fulfilling her role correctly. She should not wait until her appraisal or until the subject comes up as part of her professional development as this may not happen for some time. If she is not successful in approaching either of these individuals Myra may wish to speak to the Deputy headteacher or seek advice from colleagues who may have worked with this age group. There may also be some training or reading materials which she may be able to access. She should look online at the Statutory Framework for the Early Years Foundation Stage, which will give her guidance about the learning and development requirements as well as the practical considerations of her role.

Brilliant case study

Tina has just got a job supporting a Reception teacher working in a small school. In her first job as a teaching assistant, she was at a larger primary where the Reception and Nursery classes worked together as a unit for the foundation stage and did not have much contact with the rest of the school, particularly as they were housed in a separate building. In her new job, the school does not have a Nursery, and the Reception class are expected to join in far more with whole school activities such as assemblies. Tina is surprised by the difference and is quite unsettled as a result as she is not sure that it is appropriate for this age group.

- Do you think that this could be a problem?
- Should Tina say anything?

Solution

This could be a problem if Tina starts to voice her concerns to others in the school rather than speaking to the Foundation Stage manager or another member of the Senior Management Team. She should speak to her line manager for her own peace of mind and for reassurance in the first instance rather than saying anything negative to colleagues. She should remember that every school will be slightly different and that the headteacher should be aware of the foundation stage requirements and will have reasons for managing whole school activities in the way in which he or she has.

Brilliant case study

Neil is an experienced teaching assistant who is working with a newly qualified or early career teacher (ECT) in Year 8. They have been working well throughout the autumn term and the teacher sends Neil her plans each week in advance. However, on looking through the maths plans for the following week, Neil has noticed that she is aiming to deliver an ambitious lesson to the group which he knows that some of the pupils he supports are going to struggle with.

- Should Neil say something and if so, what?
- How can this situation be managed sensitively if these kinds of issues continue?

Solution

Neil should definitely say something but will need to approach this situation sensitively so as not to undermine the teacher. He could try something like, 'I worked on this with these children in Year 7 and they had a lot of difficulty understanding the concept – would it be worth taking them back over what we did last year first?'

Neil's teacher will be working closely with a mentor as she is newly qualified, so if these kinds of issues continue it is likely that they will become apparent as the year goes on and be managed appropriately.

Brilliant case study

Ann has been asked to work within the biology department at her secondary school as there are not enough support staff for this area. Although she has studied the subject at school herself this was a long time ago and she does not feel confident enough to support pupils in biology. She usually works in the geography and PE departments.

- What might be a good starting point for Ann?
- How could she use support available within the school and beyond to support her knowledge and skills?

Solution

Ann should start by thinking about her current level of knowledge and skills in the subject and then speak to other support staff who work within the biology department. This will help her to get an idea of what is expected rather than imagining ideas which may not be correct! She should also ask whether she can sit in on a couple of lessons as an extra support assistant so that she can gain further insight into how the subject is supported. The department as a whole may be able to offer further support as may any training courses.

Chapter 3

Brilliant case study

Rosanna is working with a group of Year 8 pupils on some long division problems. One of the group, Mikey, is telling her that he can't do it and doesn't understand it as there are too many things to remember.

- What could Rosanna say to Mikey?
- How might the use of scaffolding help in this situation?
- Why will this also benefit Mikey in the future?

Solution

The pupils should have some strategies that they can use when they become stuck in their learning, and Rosanna may need to remind them of these first. For example, looking at the learning objective and thinking about exactly what they have been asked to do, or looking around the classroom for any resources or learning materials which might help him. Rosanna should then reassure Mikey and tell him that practising problem solving in class will help him to remember the different steps to follow. Scaffolding might help, and Rosanna should ask Mikey if he can remember the first step to use when looking at a problem and then support and encourage him through questioning him about the different stages in the process. This will also benefit Mikey in the future as he will be able to think independently about how to work through a problem.

Brilliant case study

Jamal is supporting in Year 1 and has recently started working in a new school. He is an experienced assistant and has always kept stickers in his pocket to hand out to pupils. During maths, he notices that one girl is trying particularly hard and gives her a sticker. Later on the class teacher tells Jamal that stickers are never used in that particular school and that verbal praise is seen as far more powerful. Jamal is very surprised.

- What do you think about Jamal's reaction?
- Is anyone in the wrong here?
- What else could Jamal do the next time he sees the girl trying hard?

Solution

Jamal's reaction is understandable but it is important in this situation that someone in the school should take him through both the behaviour policy and also the rewards which the school uses for promoting effort. This should have been explained to him when he started in his role so it is not Jamal's fault – schools need to have clear guidelines for staff concerning the kinds of rewards which they can use. The next time Jamal sees the girl trying hard he should reward her with praise, tell the teacher and follow school policy.

Brilliant case study

Andre has been asked to work with a group of six Year 7 pupils on a regular basis to focus on developing their basic maths skills as they need additional support. He has been given a list of the skills that they need to work on but has not had any more information from the maths teacher.

- What further information should Andre be given?
- Why is it important that Andre is given appropriate support when working with this group?

Solution

Before starting to work with the group, Andre should know the results of any assessments which the teacher has carried out with the pupils, so that he has a starting point. Any individual maths targets which the pupils have would also be helpful so that he can tie these in where possible. He should then be given a series of lesson plans or structured intervention sessions so that he knows how to build on the pupils' learning. It is important that Andre is given appropriate support so that the pupils can gain maximum benefit from the intervention sessions.

Brilliant case study

Andi has been asked to observe a Year 3 child on the playground and has been told that staff have raised concerns about him. However Andi is not clear on exactly what she is looking for or how to record it.

- Why is it important that Andi is clear on the purpose of the observation?
- What kind of information would be helpful for Andi?

Solution

It is important that Andi is clear on the purpose of the observation as she will not know what she is looking for, and the session will not benefit the pupil or give the right information to teachers. Andi should know what type of observation she is carrying out, how long she should be observing and specifically what she is looking for, as well as how her observation should be recorded.

Chapter 4

Brilliant case study

Pushra works as a teaching assistant in the Reception class in a small primary school. She is completing an early years qualification and as part of the course is looking at effective safeguarding practice. She realises that the school have not given her any information or training on safeguarding since she started in her role.

- Describe what Pushra should do.
- Why is it important that she takes some action?

Solution

Pushra should speak to her teacher or line manager to let them know that she has not been given the school's safeguarding policy or had any information about it. All schools have a legal duty to safeguard and promote the welfare of children and young people and to make staff aware of their responsibilities. She could also look online herself to see whether she can read the policy. It is very important that she takes some action as all school staff should know the correct steps to take when they have safeguarding concerns.

Brilliant case study

Jack is working as a cover supervisor in key stage 3. He does not work with all the pupils as he tends to cover maths and music lessons, but this involves working with the same pupils each week. He has been approached by a pupil in Year 9 who has said that she is worried about her friend in her class whose father is an alcoholic – she says that her friend has confided in her that he is sometimes violent with both her and her mother.

- Outline what Jack should do.
- What should he say to each of the girls about the situation?

Solution

Jack should speak to the DSL as soon as possible and tell them exactly what the girl has said to him. He should also make written notes in case there is any further need to remember details. He should respond to the girl who has spoken to him by saying that she has done the right thing in telling him and that he will help her friend. He should not ask too many questions or take the matter into his own hands by going to speak to her himself.

Brilliant case study

Jean-Paul works in a small village primary school where the pupils usually transfer to a number of much larger secondary schools in the area. He spends his time as a teaching assistant in a mixed Year 5/6 class and is presently working with the teacher to manage the leavers' production and to ensure that the transition process goes smoothly.

- Why is it particularly important in Jean-Paul's school to manage transition actively and to reassure pupils about any concerns which they may have?
- How might Jean-Paul be involved in the process?

Solution

It is important for all schools to manage the transition from primary to secondary school actively but for a smaller primary, especially when feeding much larger secondary schools, it will help pupils to be able to discuss what their new surroundings will be like and how teaching and learning will be different. They should also have opportunities to visit the school and discuss issues such as travelling to school, managing homework and organisation skills. Jean- Paul may be involved in the process in a number of ways, from taking out individuals or small groups to discuss worries that they may not want to talk about in front of the class, to working with Year 7 teachers to discuss common issues.

Brilliant case study

Leanne is a teaching assistant in Years 5 and 6. The school nurse has come to speak to Year 6 about puberty and what they can expect to happen. The talk is happening separately for boys and girls. Some of the children have said to Leanne that they do not need to go to the talk as they already know what is going to happen as part of puberty.

- What should Leanne say to the children?
- Why is it important that they go to the talk?

Solution

Leanne should tell the children that they may know about some of what is happening but that they may not know everything. She should tell them that they will have the opportunity to ask any questions which come up as part of the conversation. It is important for them to go to the talk to ensure that all the children have the same information.

Brilliant case study

Joseph is in your class in Reception and has always been happy and settled. However, for the past week his behaviour has been very different. He has been unable to concentrate on anything and has been repeatedly pushing other children and taking things away from them. The teacher has asked his mum to come in after school to talk about his behaviour and she tells her that Joseph's father moved out last week and that her boyfriend has moved into their home.

- Why is it important for the teacher to talk this through with Joseph's mum?
- How can you and the teacher support Joseph?

Solution

It is important for the teacher to talk this through with Joseph's mum as she may not be aware that the changes at home can have an effect on his behaviour; he is likely to be reacting to the departure of his father and will need support from the adults around him. The teacher should suggest a meeting with the SENDCo to find out how they can do this and to look at the support that is available, as well as finding ways to help Joseph both at home and in school.

Chapter 5

Brilliant case study

Year 5 have been in the class for almost half a term and the class teacher and teaching assistant have devised an agreed set of rules with the children which are displayed on the wall. There have been a number of issues within the class between the children and one particular child, Ralf, seems to be at the centre of most of the incidents. The class teacher says to him, 'Ralf, we agreed as a class that we will always be kind to others.'

- Do you think that that Ralf will be more likely to listen to the teacher since he helped devise the rules?
- What else could staff do to try to ensure that this kind of behaviour occurs less frequently?

Solution

Ralf should be more likely to listen to the teacher as he helped to agree the set of rules which are on display. It may be necessary to remind him of this whilst talking about how his behaviour will have made his friend feel. If his behaviour carries on it may be necessary to speak to the SENDCo about how to help him to manage his feelings.

Staff in the classroom should reinforce the class rules by drawing the attention of the children to them regularly and by praising the behaviour of those who are observing them, for example 'Well done Axel for lining up quietly'. It will also be helpful to have a whole school policy for behaviour management so that all staff know the kinds of rewards to use alongside verbal praise.

Brilliant case study

Josh is in Year 7 and is struggling to manage his behaviour. This takes the form of regular fights during breaktimes, and frustration and loud name calling within the classroom. The SENDCo has asked his parents to come in for a meeting with his form teacher and year group leader and it is clear that his father, who does most of the parenting due to his mother's long work hours, is very strict with Josh at home.

- What type of parenting style is being demonstrated here?
- Do you think that it is the cause of Josh's poor behaviour in school?
- How might the school and Josh's parents work together to support him?

Solution

An authoritarian parenting style is likely to be demonstrated here. It may be a contributing factor to Josh's behaviour, particularly if he has a strict set of rules at home and no explanation, input or understanding of their purpose. This may cause him to be frustrated and to challenge authority as there is little give and take in the home environment. The school and Josh's parents should work together through talking to him about his feelings and the purpose of having rules, as well as working out ways of giving him opportunities to make his own choices.

Brilliant case study

Marwa is in Year 9 and has recently come to your school following a house move. She has been in school for two months and there are serious concerns about her behaviour which is defiant towards adults, as she often refuses to carry out instructions or work with others. She has not responded to any of the school's strategies for managing behaviour, has not made many friends and is quite isolated during breaks. Teachers have met her mother and the SENDCo but have been told that Marwa's behaviour is fine at home although she is concerned. The school has not had Marwa's records from her previous school.

- Why might Marwa be displaying this type of behaviour in school?
- How might you and the teacher support Marwa?

Solution

It is important to try to speak to Marwa to find out what might be the cause of her behaviour. Teachers may ask you to try to get to know Marwa and to build a relationship with her – in this way she may be encouraged to talk to you. Her behaviour may be a reaction to her move but this will need to be clarified. You should always work with other staff and in particular the SENDCo to devise a support plan so that she can be supported effectively.

Brilliant case study

Sheila is working in the EYFS in her school and moves between the Nursery and Reception classes. In one of her groups is a child who regularly runs out of class, lashes out and often strikes other children and adults. The child is not able to focus on tasks or sit with other children. The class teacher has called a meeting with the child's foster parents, the SENDCo and all those who work with her.

- What might be the first steps in this situation?
- What else can the school do to support this pupil?

Solution

The first steps in this situation would be to talk to the child's parents about their behaviour so that they are aware of what is happening. They may have similar issues at home or be able to tell staff about any possible underlying reasons for the child's behaviour. The teacher and SENDCo may then discuss with parents the steps that the school are able to take in this situation, and Sheila may be involved in some of these if the child needs to be taken out of the class for some of the time to support their behaviour. They should then agree to meet at an agreed time to review the strategies which they have put in place. If these strategies do not work over time, the school may need to request an EHC needs assessment.

Brilliant case study

Amal has been working in a secondary school for four months and is based in Years 7 and 8. He has been trained in restorative justice techniques at his previous school and also speaks Hindi. There have been some cases of racist bullying amongst the girls in the two year groups during breaktimes and Amal suggests to the head of Year 7 that he should run some sessions.

- What should Amal do first?
- What kind of form could the sessions take?

Solution

Amal should make sure that he speaks to all sides concerned and be clear on exactly what has happened so that he can tackle the situation carefully. He should invite the two sides to come and discuss what has happened, and act as an interpreter in his language if needed. Depending on the number of pupils involved he may need to run several sessions with different pupils.

Chapter 6

Brilliant case study

Sue is working in a secondary school as a teaching assistant and cover supervisor. She has concerns about one of the boys in Year 8 due to his behaviour, but as Sue is based in different departments and works with different teachers, she is not sure who to discuss her concerns with.

- What should Sue do first?
- Why is it important that she says something?

Solution

Sue should speak to someone else as soon as possible and explain her concerns, giving examples of the pupil's behaviour. If she does not know who her line manager is, she should speak to another, more experienced teaching assistant or to a teacher to find out who this is. Her line manager will be able to support her and guide her as to what to do next and whether to involve the SENDCo.

Brilliant case study

Andre is working in Year 1 as a general teaching assistant. A child in the class, Phoebe, has shown some causes for concern due to her speech and language, which is also impacting significantly on her ability to learn. After some discussion with the SENDCo and Phoebe's parents they have decided to work initially on some specific language targets supported by her parents at home. Andre has been working with Phoebe three times a week for two terms on her targets but Phoebe has made little progress when they come to her review. After speaking to Phoebe's parents, the SENDCo and class teacher decide that they will refer Phoebe to a speech and language therapist for further assessment.

- If Phoebe does not progress further following speech and language therapy, what would be the next steps?

Solution

If Phoebe still does not make progress following speech and language therapy, it is likely that the therapist will recommend an EHC assessment. They will then be able to advise the school on next steps and how to best support Phoebe.

Brilliant case study

Ryan has been asked to work with three boys in Years 3 and 4 who have recently been diagnosed with autism to support their social and communication skills. He has been asked to take the group out twice a week but has not been given very much guidance from the SENDCo as to make the best use of his time. Although he has some experience, he is finding it challenging to manage the group due to the boys' behaviour and his own lack of confidence.

- What should Ryan do?
- How can he best support the boys so that they get the most out of the sessions?

Solution

Ryan should speak to the SENDCo firstly and explain the situation, as his time is valuable and should be used effectively. As he is not experienced in working with these pupils, he should highlight his lack of confidence and say that he needs more support. Ideally he should be given support from teachers or the SENDCo in the form of session planning and suggested areas of focus in this area to ensure that the sessions are productive.

Brilliant case study

You are working as an individual support assistant for Bhumika, who is in Year 5.

She is autistic and also has problems with speech and language. The autism advisory teacher comes into school once a term to observe Bhumika and to speak to you, and then separately to Bhumika's parents and the SENDCo. He writes a report which gives suggested targets for Bhumika's EHCP, which he goes through with you and always tells you that you will have a copy. However, in the eighteen months you have been at the school you have never received a copy. You have asked the SENDCo several times and although she always says that she will pass it on to you this has not happened. You can only assume that this is because she is always so busy.

- Why is it important that you should get to see the report?
- What would you do in this situation?

Solution

It is very important that you should see the report and other information concerning Bhumika's progress as you are working as her individual support assistant. You should have access to this to enable you to support her effectively. If the SENDCo does not pass on the information, ask whether you can make an appointment with her to discuss Bhumika's progress formally and make a point of outlining your concerns, if necessary with another member of staff present.

Chapter 7

Brilliant case study

A primary school is sending Year 6 on a residential trip at the end of the year to an outdoor activity centre, which they do every year. There are two pupils who have disabilities in the year group who they have now realised will be excluded from the trip as the school has not taken their needs into consideration.

- What kind of discrimination is this?
- How could the school and/or the centre make a reasonable adjustment so that the pupils can take part?

Solution

This is indirect discrimination as the needs of the two pupils should have been considered when the trip was planned.

The school should have planned a trip in which the pupils' needs were taken into account and mentioned their needs when booking. However, the centre also has a legal responsibility to ensure that activities are appropriate for all pupils and to make reasonable adjustments in the activities which they offer.

Brilliant case study

A class of Year 7 children have been asked to carry out a PE activity which they have not done before in which they have to run along a track and jump over a series of hurdles at a new local sports centre. The pupils are mainly keen although four of them think that they will not be able to do it and are saying that it would be better if they cheered the others on. As the teaching assistant, you have been asked to speak to the pupils who are lacking confidence to encourage them to have a go. You persuade them and to their surprise, one of them comes first.

- Why is it important to give all pupils the same opportunities?
- What might you have said to those who did not want to carry out the activity?

Solution

It is important to give all pupils the same opportunities so that they are able to develop their skills and to give them support to meet their potential.

To those who did not want to carry out the activity, you might encourage them by saying that it's always good to try new things because they might find that they like them, and that nobody will judge them for getting it wrong.

Brilliant case study

You are working in a Reception class and Irena has started school alongside other children. Her parents are Latvian and she speaks Latvian at home with her family so her English has been learned at Nursery and from the TV. As a result, Irena's English is less well developed than her Latvian although she does speak both languages. Her mother asks you and the class teacher for advice to encourage Irena to develop her spoken English.

- What should you say to Irena's mother?
- How could you support Irena in developing her spoken English?

Solution

Irena's mother should not be overly concerned as now she is in school she is likely to pick up English quite quickly; however, it would be wise for the school to monitor her language development in English to make sure that this is the case. She is likely to be learning English more slowly than Latvian as she does not speak it at home. Irena's family should continue to speak Latvian to her. You could support her language development by playing games and talking to Irena about different activities when she is carrying them out so that you help to develop her vocabulary.

Brilliant case study

Bohdan came to the UK from Ukraine at the start of the war. He has been in the UK for two years but has had to switch schools due to a house move. He has just arrived in your school in Year 8 and is not speaking at all, although it is clear he understands most of what is being said. Your school has not yet received any records from his previous school.

- What could be done to find out more about Bohdan's situation?
- How can the school develop more of an idea of his language needs?

Solution

The SENDCo should work with Bohdan's parents or carers to talk through what is happening and to try to support him emotionally as another change is likely to have been challenging for him. This will also help the school to gather more information about his language needs and find out what kind of support should be put in place. If his parents do not speak English, they may need access to a translator.

Brilliant case study

Sobiga is a new pupil in your class who does not speak any English. Although she has made friends and is involved in class activities, you have noticed that at breaktimes and lunchtimes she is often on her own.

- What kind of support does Sobiga need and why?
- List some strategies that you could use to help her to develop her confidence and language skills.

Solution

Sobiga needs to have some support in developing her friendships and confidence in using social language outside the classroom. It may help her on the playground or at breaks if you can encourage her to join in with playground games using equipment and facilities which are available. She could also be given a 'buddy' to look after her at these times of day. Depending on her age this may not be appropriate so if Sobiga is an older pupil you could also talk to her about going to any extra-curricular activities which are on offer at the school. The school may also offer additional support and you may be able to speak to your SENDCo or if possible an English as a second language advisory teacher about the kinds of strategies which are appropriate for her.

Chapter 8

Brilliant case study

Errol has been working in a large secondary school for two months and has been working through his induction with his line manager. However, as everyone seems very busy, he has not seen the school health and safety policy and has not had any training on it. He only realises this after the school have a fire drill and he is unsure what to do.

- Should Errol say anything?
- What else could he do in this situation?

Solution

Errol should say something to his line manager following the fire drill as the school need to ensure that all staff are aware of what to do when they need to evacuate the building. However, he should also read the health and safety policy, which should be available online or in the school office. This will give him more information about what to do.

Brilliant case study

Gina has just started a job in a new primary school. She is regularly on playground duty and notices that staff often carry cups of tea and coffee outside, particularly in colder weather. They are also able to take hot drinks to their classrooms. Gina is very alert to this as in her previous school there was an accident in which a pupil suffered serious burns after running into an adult who was carrying a hot drink. As she is new she does not wish to appear to be a killjoy; however, she is anxious that the same thing does not happen again.

- Should Gina say anything?
- Can you think of a way in which this could be resolved without upsetting other staff?

Solution

Gina should definitely say something in confidence, either to the headteacher or the school's health and safety officer. It may be that the school had not considered the dangers of allowing staff to do this. If the school then forbids carrying hot drinks she will not be seen as responsible. One suggestion is sharing break times so that two teachers cover; for example in a 20-minute break there are two ten-minute shifts to allow each person to have a drink and comfort break. Alternatively schools might decide to allow staff to carry hot drinks if they are contained in flasks or high sided boxes so that any spills do not present a hazard to others.

Brilliant case study

Carey is concerned about one of the Year 6 pupils she does a maths intervention with each day. He has recently become very withdrawn and has missed quite a bit of school. She has asked him if he is okay a couple of times but he has just shrugged and said yes. He has also expressed some anxiety about transferring to secondary school.

- Write a short list of the steps that Carey could take in this situation.

Solution

Carey should first of all speak to the class teacher in case she knows more about why the pupil may be withdrawn and whether anything has been done as yet about his absence. It is important that the teacher works with his parents to find out what the issue might be and how the school can support him. Carey could also ask the pupil about his worries regarding secondary school and talk them through, which might help him to feel less anxious. It is likely that the school will be running some sessions alongside local secondary schools which will help address some of his concerns.

Chapter 9

Brilliant case study

Saskia is an experienced support assistant and in addition has just started to run a small craft club for key stage 2 after school. She has the use of a classroom and has a group of twelve children for the activities. Saskia has taken a register of pupils at the beginning so knows who is present but following the club, one of the Year 6 children tells her that she is allowed to walk home on her own. Ten minutes later her mother comes to collect her and although she is late tells Saskia that she did not give her permission to walk home and will be speaking to the headteacher straightaway.

- How should Saskia have responded to the girl's request?
- What should she do now to support the parent?

Suggested solution

If the girl did not have written permission with her, Saskia should have asked the pupil to wait until she was able to check with the child's teacher or the school office and explain why.

It is important that she supports the parent by taking her to the headteacher and then trying to trace the girl in whatever way is decided by the group.

Brilliant case study

Rob runs the local scout group and the venue he has been using has just told him that they will be unable to carry on using it due to building work over the next few months. As he also works at the local secondary school as a member of support staff, he has had the idea of booking the school hall and also offering Duke of Edinburgh award training to pupils from the surrounding area as an extra activity.

- Would Rob be able to do this?
- Where might he go for support in order to see his idea through?

Solution

Rob may be able to do this if it is agreed by the school. He should then approach surrounding schools to gauge the level of interest – it may be that he has too many pupils to offer to a wider number. He could also talk to others in local schools who run clubs and extended schools activities for additional support and can contact them through his local authority.

Chapter 10

Brilliant case study

Jack is working as an individual support assistant for a blind pupil in a secondary school. He has been there for two years and although he is very experienced and well trained for his work with the pupil he does not have any qualifications although he has been investigating some of his options. He would like to be better qualified as there is a possibility that his pupil may be moving schools; however, he does not have much contact with his line manager as he is not full time and there are no points of contact during the week.

- What should Jack do first?
- Is there anything else he could do if the school could not support his request?

Solution

Jack should first of all speak to his line manager to find out whether the school will support him and if there is any training available. If for some reason they are unable to, for example if there is nothing available which will fit with his timetable or they are unable to let him out of school in lesson times, he may need to find out about evening classes through his local college or through the local authority. There may also be the possibility of attending online courses at a date or time to suit him.

Appendix 2: Teacher/ TA feedback sheet

Teacher/TA Feedback Sheet

To be filled in by teacher: Class:
Teacher's name:
TA's name:

Brief description of activity

How session is linked to medium-term plans

TA's role

Important vocabulary

Key learning points

For use during group work:

Children	D	H	Feedback/Assessment

D = Can do task
H = Help required to complete task

Source: Burnham, L. (2007) *S/NVQ Level 3 The Teaching Assistant's Handbook: Primary Schools*

Glossary

ADD	Attention Deficit Disorder
ADHD	Attention Deficit Hyperactivity Disorder
AEN	Additional Educational Needs
AFL	Assessment for Learning
ASD	Autistic Spectrum Disorder
BSP	Behaviour Support Plan
BTA	Bilingual Teaching Assistant
CCE	Child Criminal Exploitation
CEO	Chief Executive Officer
COP	Code of Practice
CPD	Continuing Professional Development
CPP/R	Child Protection Plan/Register
CSE	Child Sexual Exploitation
CYPMHS	Children and Young People's Mental Health Services (formerly CAMHS)
DFE	Department for Education
DLD	Developmental Language Disorder
DSL	Designated Safeguarding Lead
EAL	English as an Additional Language
ECT	Early Career Teacher (formerly NQT)
EHCP	Education and Health Care Plan
ELSA	Emotional Literacy Support Assistant
EYFS	Early Years Foundation Stage
EWO	Education Welfare Officer
EP	Educational Psychologist
FGM	Female Genital Mutilation
GDPR	General Data Protection Regulation

HLTA	Higher Level Teaching Assistant
INSET	In Service Education and Training
IEP	Individual Education Plan
ISA	Individual Support Assistant
LA	Local authority
LO	Learning objective
LSA	Learning support assistant
LSP	Local Safeguarding Partnership
MAT	Multi Academy Trust
MITA	Maximising the Impat of Teaching Assistants
NAPTA	National Association of Professional Teaching Assistants
NQT	Newly Qualified Teacher (now ECT)
OT	Occupational Therapist
PPA	Planning, Preparation and Assessment
PPE	Personal Protective Equipment
PSHE	Personal, Social and Health Education
PSP	Personal Support Plan
QTS	Qualified Teacher Status
SALT/SLT	Speech and Language Therapist
SDP	School Development Plan
SEAL	Social and Emotional Aspects of Learning
SIP	School Improvement Partner
SLCN	Speech, language and communication needs
SMT/SLT	Senior Management Team/Senior Leadership Team
SEND	Special Educational Needs and Disabilities
SENDCo	Special Educational Needs and Disabilities Co-Ordinator
SALT/SLT	Speech and Language Therapist

Index